ALSO BY I......

POETRY

Kindling
(Onlywomen Press, 1982)

Moving into the Space Cleared by Our Mothers
(Salmon, 1991)

The River That Carries Me
(Salmon, 1995)

Like Joy in Season, Like Sorrow
(Salmon, 2001)

Perhaps the Heart is Constant After All
(Salmon, 2012)

FICTION

A Noise from the Woodshed
(Onlywomen Press, 1987)

Scarlet O'Hara, a novella
(Onlywomen Press, 1993)

Biography of Desire
(Poolbeg, 1997)

salmonpoetry
*Celebrating 35 Years
of Literary Publishing*

To Air the Soul, Throw All the Windows Wide

NEW & SELECTED POEMS

Mary Dorcey

Published in 2016 by
Salmon Poetry
Cliffs of Moher, County Clare, Ireland
Website: www.salmonpoetry.com
Email: info@salmonpoetry.com

ISBN 978-1-910669-53-2

COVER PHOTOGRAPH: *"Tania" by Conor Horgan – www.conorhorgan.com*
COVER DESIGN & BOOK TYPESETTING: *Siobhán Hutson*
Printed in Ireland by Sprint Print

Salmon Poetry gratefully acknowledges the support of
The Arts Council / An Chomhairle Ealaoín

For Alexandra

Acknowledgements

The author extends her sincere gratitude to the Arts Council of Ireland, the Tyrone Guthrie Centre at Annaghmakerrig and the Centre Culturel Irlandais, Paris, for their support of her work.

Contents

from
LIKE JOY IN SEASON, LIKE SORROW (2001)

from
PERHAPS THE HEART IS CONSTANT
AFTER ALL (2012)

NEW POEMS

from
Kindling
(1982)

Woman in a Normandy Field

She stood alone
under a grey sky's impassive discipline,
dark earth stretched about her beyond sight
   its raw furrows gaping.
Turning full circle she surveyed a year's work
   laid out like a cloth behind her.
Then slowly her knees bent to ground once more
   and with deliberate hands
she began the season's first task.

Blood Relations

Leaving
she bends to kiss you
slowly on each cheek,
drawing closer to let slip
a few last words
in your foreign tongue
and I, discreet,
embarrassed to be the chosen,
the one who stays,
lower my eyes and pretend indifference
granting her one last intimacy.

Can you blame me then
if I forget,
that it is only your mother
saying goodbye after morning coffee
whose eyes as they acknowledge mine
are brilliant with shamed jealousy?

Mirrors

At the foot of your garden
The sea plunges in its narrow bed.
Stilled by its clamour you stand,

Peonies and lupin that he planted
The year of his death, each summer
Recover their place about you. You

Have grown old in their light. You
Have watched your children go from
You and said no word to halt them. You

Have friends and books – money enough
A good neighbour to one side – six
Grandchildren. But your daughters will

Never marry now and you will never
See your eyes shine from the faces of
Their daughters. This one regret

You hold in silence, for you have other
Windows to the world, through which you
Glimpse a life and loves not spoken of

In well curtained drawing rooms. I
Walk from you with my woman lover
Down the smooth flower lined path,

Your smile follows me to the gate and
No stranger passing could tell what
Dark pleasures are mirrored in your eyes.

Night

I remember your neck, its strength
and the sweetness of the skin at your throat.
I remember your hair, long, in our way
drawing it back from my mouth.
How my hands slid the low plain of your back
thrown by the sudden flaunt of your loins.
I remember your voice, the first low break
and at last the long flight
loosing us to darkness.
And your lips along my shoulder,
more sure, even than I had imagined –
how I guarded their track.

I ask you then what am I to do with all these memories
heavy and full?
Hold them, quiet, between my two hands,
as I would if I could again
your hard breasts?

Night Protest

We stood outside that prison wall,
The slow rain speared by barbed wire,
Stood outside and called your name.
Called against the dark and our own dread
In the shadow of that grey stone mass,
Where each square foot of twilight
Is held behind bars.
Then through the clouded air something

Fluttered white – a strip of sheet
Or handkerchief
Making its own small peace there
By reaching out to us.
And was it your voice that broke clear?
Two hundred stood in silence but
It did not come again.
Later a cell light flashed

Once – twice – a signal surely
Or just some careless warder?
So we sang for you the old battle songs
For you who had so often stood
On both sides of this wall,
And someone set a placard burning
Sparking a passage for our voices,
And I wanted to call *'She's still*
Carrying a torch for your Marie.'
Nell cried the last message *'We'll be*
Seeing you soon again but we have
To go home for our dinners now.'
And I thought of yours that day,
Each day – the oiled tea, damp bread,
The egg and sausage floating
On a tin plate.

And I tried not to think of those other
Abuses – the little things that cripple:
The drooling eye at the peep-hole
And two sanitary towels – per woman
– Per month.
And how many others inside that fortress
Strained to hear their own name spoken?
How many others forgotten

Unknown
In for a pound of butter
Or for servicing some man in a car.
So we sang for them too
'Oh sisters don't you weep, don't you
Moan' and maybe they knew.
We left one by one, some still calling
A name or a joke

Moving slowly for your sake
But wanting to run from the damp
Infectious air of that place.
And the 'Branch' men sullen in their
Cars, watched us pass stiff eyed
The sense beginning to grip at last,
That they'd more than one
Brazen bitch – banging the bars.

House in Winter

In a cold room
dawn light stirs on skin.
Wind sucks at the roof beams,
lip to bone we rekindle
the old track of heat along the nerves.
From hand to widening eye
the spark climbs
the taut rope of your spine.
Ribs crack like tinder.

Below us
someone moves about the empty house.
Our cupped hands hold the flame
our mouths suckle it.
Footsteps mount the stairs
shudder through our breathing.
Higher and higher – they come
stumble past the door
and quicken –

My hands fly loose
your eyes catch fire.
From heart and lungs and belly
breath sings –
the air shatters
in spears of ringing crystal
blue and gold and silver.

Somewhere below
a door slams shut
returning us.
Silence seeps like snow
about the roof and walls.
But listen –

at the window
we have startled a yellow wasp
from winter.
With a fevered hum
it climbs the chill glass
beating its way to summer.

In a cold room
we reach slowly
and draw the fallen covers
up from our feet.

from

Moving into the Space
Cleared by Our Mothers

(1991)

First Love

You were tall and beautiful.
You wore your long dark hair
wound about your head,
your neck stood clear and full
as the stem of a vase.
You held my hand in yours
and we walked slowly
talking of small familiar happenings
and of the lost secrets
of your childhood. It seems

It was always autumn then.
The amber trees shook. We
laughed in a wind that cracked
the leaves from black boughs
and set them scuffling about
our feet, for me to trample still,
then kick in orange clouds
about your face. We would climb
dizzy to the cliff's edge and
stare entranced at a green and

purple sea, the storm howling at
our ears, as it tore the breath from
white cheeked waves. You steadied
me against the wheel and screech
of gulls, I loved to think that but
for your strength I would tumble to
the rocks below to the fated death,
your stories made me dream of. I
don't remember that I looked into
your eyes or that we ever asked

An open question. our thoughts
passed through our blood, it seemed,
and the slightest pressure of our
hands decided all issues wordlessly.
We watched in silence by the shore,
our gaze misted by the chill spray,
in mutual need of the water's
fierce, inhuman company, that gave
promise of some future, timeless
refuge from all the fixed anxieties

Of our world. As we made for home
we turned into the gale, my thighs
were grazed by teeth of ice, you
gathered your coat about me and
hurried our steps towards hearth, fire
and the comfort of your sweet,
strong tea. We moved bound in step.
You sang me songs of Ireland's
sorrows and of proud women loved
and lost. I knew then, they set for me

A brilliant stage of characters, who
even now, can seem more intimate
than my most cherished friends.
We walked together, hand in hand.
You were tall and beautiful, you wore
your long brown hair wound about
your head, your neck stood clear and
full as the stem of a vase. I was
young, you were my mother and it
seems it was always autumn then.

Hands

An old woman is working
in a garden
raking dead leaves
from the earth;

back bent to uncover
the first growth
of a new season.

Will I not see you again?
My blood cannot believe it
— though I have chosen.

You talk too much
— think too much, you said
as I did, and do.
I love
— I loved your hands
that were never still
shaped to their own purpose
by the shaping of things.

Your hands that were not cruel.
The tongue wounds at a slip;
eyes in a glance
or the refusal of it
tear at the heart's root.
But your hands made a silence
wherever they touched,
a stopping place —
the first before love.

The evenings lengthen –
light holds on
for hours in the sky.
Time wipes it all clear
they say, all but
a way of standing
the timbre of a voice.

Thinking of talking –
I wait for night
at a window.

I spread my hands, empty
on the pane –
hands almost still.
I watch an old woman
working –
turning up new soil
in a garden.

In the City of Boston

I have seen mad women in my time,
I have seen them waiting row on row,
I have seen the stripped flesh,
the abandoned eye,
I have seen the frothing mouth
and heard the cries,
I have seen mad women in my time
– I have never seen them mad enough.

In the city of Boston I once saw a woman
and she was mad – as mad as they come
(and oh do they come, mad women,
as often as the rest?)
She walked the street in broad daylight,
neat as a pin – a lady no doubt
in blue coat, blue hat, blue purse
blue shoes – the only note
out of place in it all
was her face – the peculiar angle
of her head; thrown back, jaws wide
and a scream so shrill poured out,
it lifted the birds from her feet.

Sunshine in an elegant Boston square
choc-a-block with the office lot
loosed to eat,
no one turned, no one stared
from their clean cut day,
nobody cared to embarrass the mad.
She strode through that crowd
sealed tight in her mind,
chin high, clutching her bag,
her terrible siren full on.

Mechanical agony guided her step
until she reached the pavement's edge.
There at the crossroads
– an extraordinary thing –
her polished shoes halted,
she lowered her head,
the animal howl died in her throat –
stock still, patient, ordered
she stood
because the traffic light was red.

I have seen mad women in my time,
I have seen them burn
the skin from their breasts,
I have seen them claw a lover's eyes,
I have seen the blade across the bone,
have seen the frothing mouth
and heard the moan –
I have seen the abandoned faces
row on row,
I have seen mad women in my time
– I have never seen us mad enough.

Not Everyone Sees This Night

The first frost
has brought back summer.
Walking in the garden
my feet crack the whitened grass —
the smell is of hay —
just cut.

They ask me
if I'm happy here —
they ask
as if used to answers.

The sky is luminous and vast
more blue than day;
it cannot hold its stars —
they spill wide and down
I hear them fall
behind the black mountains.

No one has seen such a moon.

The silence is the loudest thing:
breath roars out —
a milky stream,
and yes —
a moment later
from off stage —
comes the sea.
They ask me
if I'm happy here.

A dog bays to stretch the quiet.
Two miles off
a neighbour's light
goes dark.
The cats forsake the hearth
to roll
spring madness
on the spiked crunch
of earth.

Beneath its slates
the house huddles –
yellow eyes gleaming.
The mallow in blossom
purple at the gate.

Sometimes when I go in
you are asleep –
your bed under the skylight.
Sometimes I do not wake you.

Not everyone sees
this night –
there are others –
here
and elsewhere.
Not everyone
sleepless in these hours,
watching for dawn
regrets its coming.

I pluck the ice cold grass –
a handful
and go indoors.

I hold it to my lips
before I kiss you
so that when I do
your lips –
burn.

Deliberately Personal

Who is the woman
who drove the children to school
made the beds and washed the dishes –
who hoovered the wall-to-wall carpet –
before slitting her throat at the bathroom mirror?

Who is the man
who drove his favourite niece to the party
in her flowered pink frock –
in her ribbons and bows;
who raped her on the back seat
on the way back –
Why not? he said
look how she was dressed?
and besides –
hadn't she been doing it for years
with her father?

Who are these people –
where do they come from?
What kind of man –
what kind of woman?
Where do they live –
who lives next door to them?
How come none of us
ever knows them?

And how is it;
wherever it happens –
he doesn't belong to us?
How is it he's always
somebody else's
brother, father, husband?

Why is it
whoever she is
she's never more
than a name in the papers –
some vagrant, friendless
unnatural woman?

And who are you
come to that?
All of you
out there
out of the spotlight –
out for a night's entertainment,
smiles upturned so politely;
asking me
why I have to be –
so raw
and deliberately
personal?

Daughter

And you my daughter
who I will not know —
I feel in mine
your small, hot hand.
I see your green eyes
lighting already
with my mother's far away look,
and the kisses
that might have made you
from my lover's warm, dark lips
smiling from yours —
made for kisses.

My little daughter
what times we shall have —
what talks.
I would hold up the stars
to keep from burning you
quiet the sea
to keep from waking you.
I would eat you for breakfast
all your fat, buttery flesh
thighs and arms
toast and honey.

My little daughter —
you will not have the chance
to jail me with your tenderness
grow high and lovely
from my shrinking hide.
We will not now
confront each other
barter, threaten, promise
we will not curse each other
win or lose
my darling
we have no time for that.

I will bequeath you
little –
some words
angry, loving, careful
set down to make a space for you.

I will leave you
flowers and flame
scorched earth, black water
blue skies, laughter
hungry children
women working, loving
fire and ice –
bombs and books.

I will leave you
my daughter
this whole wide world
that was not yet
wide enough for me
to bear you into.

Return

At last, the train will lurch in,
twenty minutes past the hour, the
dark flesh of the hills, heaved behind –
before us, the narrowing fields,
the layered clouds, drifting
beyond – lit for some other advent.
And everything will conspire
against me: luggage and children
crowding the aisle. A white haired
woman, home from England,

Awkward with haste, will labour
her case to the door, her floral
print dress, a last check between me
and my first glimpse of you.
And there you are – by the turnstile
I will see you come through, though you
miss me; your brilliant eyes in flight
along the carriage windows.
You will wear your red, linen shirt,
the sleeves turned back and snatched

From the hedgerows as you drove
a swathe of flowers in your arms.
(Such a trail strewn behind us – a trail
of departures and pardons.) And my
blood will betray me – the old response,
I will hesitate, as if there might
still be time to change course,
or simply, not wanting to be caught
waiting for your gaze? The sky
will shift as I step out, a handful

Of sun thrust down on your hair.
On the narrow platform, our hips
will draw close, we will not mind
how they stare – the aggrieved faces
such a fuss –
for a woman!
And in that moment – your laughter,
the heat of your neck at my mouth,
it will all be behind me again,
I swear, as though coming home –
as though for the first time.

The Ordinary Woman

And again you ask me why –
Why don't I write a poem about
The ordinary woman?
Not the extreme, individual case,
But the normal woman, the average woman
The everyday woman?

The woman in the street
The woman in the field
The woman who works in a factory
The woman who works on a farm
The woman who has never heard of a factory
The woman who has never seen a field.

The woman who stays at home
The woman who has no home
The woman who raises children
The woman who can have no children
The woman who has too many children
The woman who wants no children.

The healthy woman   the sick woman
The growing woman   the dying woman
The menstruating woman   the menopausal woman
The married woman   the spinster woman
The woman on the make
The woman on the shelf.

The woman who works in a school
The woman who dropped out of school
The woman who never got into school.
The woman who works as a nurse
The woman who cooks for the nurse
The woman who cleans the kitchen

Where they cook for the nurse.
The woman who works in a shop every day
The woman who shops every day
The woman who shops for food
The woman who shops for clothes, for perfume
The woman who shoplifts

For clothes, for perfume.
The woman who is paid to catch
The woman who does not pay
For clothes   for food.
The career woman   the poetess woman
The mother earth woman   the charwoman

The amazon woman   the society woman
The sportswoman   the little woman
The woman who runs   the woman who walks
The woman who is on the run
The woman who has never walked.
The woman who drives a car

The woman who drives her husband's car.
The pampered woman   the kept woman
The sheltered woman   the battered woman
The victimised woman   the violent woman
The woman nobody wants
The woman who had it coming.

The woman who went sane
The woman who stayed mad
The woman who carries a gun
The woman who is shot by a gun
The woman with too much past
The woman with too little future.

The woman ahead of her times
The woman behind the times
The woman with no time.
The outdated rural woman
The alienated suburban woman
The overcrowded urban woman.

The woman who reads the news
The woman who has never made the news
The woman who starves herself to look right
The woman who starves.
The houseproud woman   the tinker woman
The family woman   the deserted woman

The illegitimate woman   the certified woman
The consumer woman   the alien woman
The emigrant woman   the immigrant woman
The decent woman   the fallen woman
The mother of his children   and
The other woman.

The articulate woman   the illiterate woman
The bluestocking woman   the ignorant woman
The deaf woman   the blind woman
The loud woman   the dumb woman
The big woman   the petite woman
The flatchested woman

The look at those tits woman
The ugly woman   the femme fatale woman
The feminine woman   the masculine woman
The painted woman   the naked woman
The lilywhite and the scarlet woman.
The woman who thinks too much

The woman who never had time to think.
The woman who fights the system
The woman who married the system
The woman who swims against the tide
The woman who swells the tide that drowns
The woman who swims against it.

The woman who sends her sons to kill
The sons of other women.
The woman who sees her daughters
Murdered by the sons of other women.
The woman who is capitalised
The woman who is communised

The woman who is colonised
The woman who is terrorised
The woman who is analysed
The woman who is advertised
The woman who is fertilised
The woman who is sterilised.

The woman who is locked in
The woman who is locked out
The woman in a prison cell
The woman in a convent cell
The woman who keeps her place
The woman who has no place.

The woman who loved her father too much
The woman who loved her mother too much
The woman who hates men
The woman who loves men
The woman who hates women
The woman who loves women.

The natural woman   the perverted woman
The veiled woman   the virgin woman
The celibate woman   the prostitute woman
The jewish woman   the buddhist muslim catholic
Hindu protestant woman
The french woman   the irish woman

The chinese woman   the indian woman
The african woman   the american woman.
The upperclass   upper middle class
Middle class   lower middle class
Upper working class   working class
Lower working class   the no class woman.

The who ever heard of her woman?
The who the hell is she woman?
The who the hell does she think she is woman?
The chaste woman   the frigid woman
The vamp the tramp and the nymphomaniac woman
The wholesome woman   the homely woman

The easy woman   the tight assed woman
The ball breaking   cock teasing
Doesn't know what she's made for woman.
The selfish woman   the martyred woman
The sluttish woman   the fussy woman
The loose woman   the uptight woman

The naive woman   the paranoid woman
The passive woman   the dominant woman
The silly woman   the hard woman
The placid woman   the angry woman
The sober woman   the drunken woman
The silent woman   the screaming woman

Yes, that's it – that's the one
Why don't you write a poem for her –
The ordinary woman?

Come Quietly or the Neighbours Will Hear

Have you ever made love
with the t.v. on
– to spare the neighbours
landlady   lord –
the embarrassment,
the joy undisguised
of two people;
especially women
(imagine the uproar)
coming together?

Come quietly
or the neighbours will hear.

That year was the worst
an aching winter of it –
small minds and towns
rented rooms and narrow beds,
walled in by other people's
decencies
and at every sitting down
to table,
broadcast at breakfast
dinner and tea
the daily ration
of obscenity.
Have you ever
made love with the t.v. on?

Come quietly
or the neighbours will hear.

On a dark evening
autumn cloths spread for tea,
fires lit.
In the wet gardens
leaves falling
on a dark evening

at last alone
a space, hungry with wanting
waiting, a fire catching
we fell –
skin in firelight burning
fell the long fall
to grace, to the floor.
On a dark evening
night coming softly in the wet gardens.

Come quietly
or the neighbours will hear.

Mouth at my breast
hands ringing in my flesh
when the Angelus rang
from the t.v. screen.
The angel of the Lord
declared unto Mary
and she conceived of the Holy Ghost
the earth, the sun and the seas.
Hail Mary   Holy Mary.
Be it done unto me according
to thy word
Hail Mary, and oh –
the sweetness of your breath –
the breath of your sweetness.

Come quietly
or the neighbours will hear.

And the word was made flesh
and dwelt amongst us.
Hands   skin   mouth   thighs
in the bedrock of flesh
sounding,
fields flooded
blood uncoursed.
Blessed art thou
and blessed is the fruit
of thy womb.

Bitter and sweet
earth opens   stars collide.
Blessed and sweet,
the fruit
among women
Hail Mary   Holy Mary.

Come quietly
or the neighbours will hear.

When the six o'clock news
struck.
Into the fissures
of mind   and bone
the deadly tide
seeping.
The necessary,
daily litany.
Come quietly or the neighbours
will hear.

She was found
on a park bench   backstreet   barn
dancehall   schoolyard   bedroom   bar —
found with multiple stab wounds to
thighs breast and abdomen.
Come quietly   come quietly
or the neighbours …
hands tied behind her back,
no sign of
(mouth bound)
no sign of
sexual assault.

Come softly
or the neighbours will hear.

Your breast and belly,
your thighs,
your hands behind my back
my breath in yours.
No one heard her scream.
Your eyes wide.
Come quietly or the neighbours ...
She was found
at the dockside   river bank,
in the upstairs flat
his flat
wearing a loose ...
your mouth at my ear.

Come quietly
or the neighbours will hear.
Blood on the walls
and sheets,
a loose negligée
in her own flat,
stripped to the waist.
Come quietly, come quietly.
No one heard her scream –
come softly or the neighbours ...
Did you ever make love
with the t.v. on?
– the neighbours heard nothing –
she was always –
no one would have thought –
always a quiet girl.

Stripped to the bone
blood on our thighs
my hands behind your back
come quietly, come –
legs tangled with the sheet
mouth to mouth
voices flung.

Come softly
or the neighbours will hear.

Did you ever make love
with the t.v. on?
to spare the neighbours
landlady lord –
her cries in our ears
we came …
no one heard her scream
her blood on our hands.
Yes –
coming,

Not quietly –
beyond bearing;
in the face of the living
in the teeth of the dying
forgetting the uproar
the outrage –
(imagine –
the joy
undisguised
of two women
– especially
women –)
two women
together –
at last alone
night falling in the wet gardens
on a dark evening
with the t.v.
off.

Die quietly –
die quietly –
or the neighbours will hear.

Repossession

They took out your womb
this year.
You had no use for it.
Every few hours
its memory
bloodies your cheek
as if you were fifty again.

You are stooped and frail
and thin
your fingers swollen
your knees don't work.

You who swung me high –
my chariot –
my tree house.

To think that once
your flesh
was fat and full enough
to feed me
to think you suckled me –
to think I broke from your body
wet and dark –
sleek as a seal's head
breaking water.

As the days draw in
your mind mislays everything
but the past.
Wanting the stairs
you walk into the kitchen.
Time slips through your fingers
you sort old treasures;
guilt and lost chances –
your own mother
who died in a Home

because you had
all of us
children
to think of.

Becalmed at your fireside —
you talk to her
and she talks back —
endlessly sifting
the argument.
Hour by hour
she reclaims you.
She has grown into your lapses —
into your hands
into your walk.

Like mother — like daughter
I say: excuses — justification.
And standing to clear the table
impatient of all this blather
I catch sight of myself
in the mirror —
the gilt-framed glass
that she left you
and oh —
there you are
reflected
already —
fitting new quarters
looking out from
my eyes.

Trying On for Size

Capsized on the bed you roll, cane white
legs treading the air. You are pulling on
your stockings, easier now this way than to
stand upright and bend. You are laughing
because I've caught you at it, one of your
secret stratagems. On the beach in summer,

Years ago, when you were young, in August,
a careless hero for an hour, your limbs
long and full, your shoulders broad, intent
on freedom, land and charges cast off, you
swam with mighty strokes out so far, we
watched in awe until your beauty was a

Bird or buoy dancing between waves. With
each new day behind us, do you remember
when, you ask. And, I do, almost all of it
and more. You were not in all moods good,
you threatened with a wooden spoon –
cursed me when there was no one else

To curse. Moored in a kitchen that over-
heard wild ocean you did not always
counsel or console. How often did your
gaze flinch from trouble, knowing too
well, the weight of grief uncomforted.
But you had a window looking south, books

To read by evening light, a work-store of
song. You named these one by one as grace
and stood them against storm. Going down
the stairs in present days, our shoes fitted
to your contrary, infant gait, I want to pick
you up and carry you or launch you along

The bannister as you did me, in this house
where we played, making up childhood
together. But the time has run out or arrived.
Now you must take every step first across
this passage. We daughters follow after,
each one moving into the space cleared by

Our mothers. And with what fine nerve, what
unthanked poise, you confront this last world
you will discover before me. I catch your shy,
jaunty smile at the mirror: See you say –
what do you think? As if death were a foolish,
extravagant hat you were trying on for size.

When You're Asleep

I'm worn out with you.

All day long
fetching and carrying
upstairs and downstairs
my back broken
picking up after you
forever under my feet.

Upstairs   downstairs
your questions trailing me
never quiet for two
minutes together –

How old were you the year that we went …?
Do you remember the time
somebody said …?
Wasn't it grand the first
summer we saw …?
Were you born yet
the last winter your father and I …?
Just let me tell you once more –
I know I've told you already …

I'm worn out with you.

But for you these are festival
days;
days you can talk
all day long
out loud for a change
morning to night,
banqueting
because I'm here
to listen.

As the hours journey
from one meal to another
I hear my voice give out
an old litany:
Eat up now
stop talking
your food will be cold.
Mind the stairs
don't hurry ... you'll fall ...

Fasten your buttons
put on your slippers
watch where you're going
come on now – we're late ...
wash yourself quickly
get into bed
it's all hours already.
Pull up your covers ...
Yes –
I'll leave the door open ...
At last you're quiet
at last it's over –
all over again
until tomorrow
and I'm too tired
to kiss you or say goodnight.

Free –
I can go downstairs
read a book
or watch television.

I'm worn out with you.

Last of all
I look in
to see if you're sleeping –
your head sunk in the pillows
so still and so small ...
when did it grow so small?
I draw close

breath held
to catch yours —
and yes,
there it is —
softly, your mouth
almost smiling
the cat curled at your shoulder.

And I'm returned
thirty years or more
when I would call out
at night
as you closed the door
to hold you there
one moment longer.
Do you love me still?
I'd sing;
and back came the same answer
always —
When you're asleep!

It Has Rained All Night While We Slept

Women have given birth
in fields
while we slept.
While we slept
women have given birth.

The mountains are huge.
A wall of iron around my heart.
The lakes, bitter black pools.
Women have drowned
in water, shallow as a basin.
Women have drowned their babies
in water no deeper
than a pool or basin
while we slept.

It has rained all night.
We wake to find it
heavy as snowfall on the window
the fields drenched with it
the earth, the stones, the leaves.
It has gouged streams
glittering
along the mountain side.

And while we slept
somewhere else –
a child has died.
Somewhere else
while we sleep
some woman's child dies
every hour
that we sleep.

Somewhere else
the split, yellow earth
littered with their bodies
dark skin, white bones

that lie quiet
as snow lies in the ruined fields.
Every hour dying
while we sleep
here,
the rain falling.
We have grown used to it.
We do not hear
the rain falling.

We know them well –
these women and their children
– or their faces.
We have grown used to them.
They follow us about
from billboards
buses
and dentists' waiting rooms –
framed in magazines
and television sets.
Eyes beautiful and blank.
Bellies – oh, bellies
big and taut
as a cow's udder.
Their hands reaching
open mouthed
to no one in particular.

All night
the rain has fallen
covering our sleep like snow.
And somewhere –
oh, somewhere out of camera –
the eyes that would not
turn from us
have closed at last.
The sweet
pitiless eyes
have shut,
disturbing
for a moment –
while we slept –

the blow-flies.

from
The River That Carries Me
(1995)

Teach Me to Remember

Teach me to remember
a Spanish town —
white cups, strong coffee,
shutters drawn in late afternoon
against the flight of swallows.
Teach me to remember
a house overlooking western seas;
the shifting light
on stone and pasture.

Music on high starred
winter nights;
opening the door
to find sheep lured
from the mountains
to listen.
Picking wild flowers in summer:
flag iris, bog cotton
carried home by the armful.

Talking politics
at breakfast,
shopping for dinner
in small country towns;
driving home through dark streets
in silence
rain falling
your hand on my knee.
You want me to learn
not to want
but I'm not good at it.
I don't know how
to half want
or half forget.

Can you teach me how to remember
a beach at evening,
the gorse in full bloom
the sky livid;
we two walking
and not remember your arm
slipping through mine –
the exact touch of your skin
at the elbow
as it slides against mine?
Snow on a roof under moonlight,
a poppy growing wild at the roadside.
The way your breath catches
with joy,
with surprise.

Teach me to remember
a village in Greece,
the sheep belling their passage
through the fields,
and you,
without a word of the language
making a friend of
every old woman
and child in the streets.
You who are moderate in nothing;
who never knew what a line was –
much less where to draw it,
will you teach me?
Someone must.

Teach me to remember
without wanting it back.

I Cannot Love You as You Want to be Loved

I cannot love you
as you want to be loved –
without wanting.
I cannot love you
without loving your black startled eyes –
without wanting them to look at me.
Without wanting to see them
catch fire
as they look at me.

I cannot love you
without loving your thighs –
the long lovely line of your thighs.
Without wanting to run my hand
along the length of them.
I cannot love you
without loving your hands –
so strong, so talkative.
Without wanting them to touch me,
to touch my hand,
my thigh.
I cannot love you as you want to be loved –
without wanting.

You are a blade
I have lifted from my own hand
to put a stop to wounding.
Who made you so sharp,
so dangerous?
I miss your laughter
and your flights of fancy.
Your foolishness,
your wild untamable ways.
I miss your passion for things –
your refusal to take life quietly.

You are a blade
I have lifted from my own hand
to put a stop to wounding.
Who made you so sharp?
so dangerous?
You whose love words
were like a bounty;
a burst of grace,
oiled and perfumed –
each one a healing,
a benediction.
You whose eyes were pools
stars might bathe in.

You are a knife
I have lifted from my own hand
to put a stop to wounding.
You should be the earth I lie down upon,
the river that carries me,
the bright sky that covers me,
the wind that sings through the lilac.
Who made you a blade
I cannot dare to handle?

Learning to Live With It

They took my pulse
and my temperature.
They told me to lie down
and be sensible.

They said all things,
bad and good come to an end.
Half a lifetime of love –
let it be enough for you.

They said I must study the alphabet –
and learn to read the writing on the wall.
They said I must come to face facts –
they handed me the blindfold.

They said I must stop listening
for the last cry from the wilderness.
They said I must stop asking –
they showed me how to cut out my tongue.

And you? Well, you, they said,
always made too much of things.
They saw the blood slipping from your eyes –
they offered you their handkerchief.

When the flesh withered on your frame
and your cheeks grew haggard
They said: See – how shapely she is –
what fine bones!

They told me to lie down and be sensible.
They said all things come to an end.
I must stop listening, they said,
for the last cry from the wilderness.

I must stop searching through grains of sand
for one grain of sand.
I must stop holding out bare arms
to stem the tide.

And when you cried out in your sleep –
Love me still love, my only love
They said: See –
she's learning to live with it!

The Making of Poetry

I will have to stop this,
I told myself
– this making of phrases;
this word spinning,
if all that inspires it
is grief.

And not that
I wasn't joyous,
often –
even careless
in that time.
But writing will not be shaped
from the surface happiness of mood.

Pleasure
like sorrow
must seep
down
to lodge in the marrow,
before
filtered,
it rejoins the bloodstream
and courses back
to feed the heart
and poetry.

This Day I have Turned my Back on Sorrow

Enough of this.
I have had enough of repining,
of loss and lament.

Enough.
I want to dance in the street.
I want laughter –
loud days and wild nights.
I will make it up,
if I have to
until it happens.
I will make it happen
if I have to.

I have had enough of repenting,
of loss
and lament.
I want
dancing in the streets,
laughter.

I will go into the fields
and under a white hawthorn tree
dig a grave
six foot deep.
Into it I will put
regret and remorse.
I will cover it up,
shovel the clay
and lay down my cross.

I have had enough
of lament
and loss.
After all
I wrote my own story,
chose my course.
I brought myself
to this edge of this river.

Enough.
It is over;
the sad times
the bleak.
Put behind me.
I have taken what I need —
the few things of value
salvaged from the wreck.
I carry them in my flesh and blood
until the last day.

Enough of loss and lament.
I want to dance in the street
I want laughter
luminous mornings, long nights.
It is over
finished,
remorse and lament
I have buried them,
turned the clay
six foot deep, under
the white hawthorn tree.

This day
I have turned my back
on sorrow.

Taking Shelter

We were talking by the lake,
engaged in formal conversation
when the rain began.

We stopped for a moment under a tree.
Not much shelter but enough.
Looking out across water
towards the darkening hills;
without pausing in your talk
you caught up your hair
and with quick hands
began to wind it about your head.
(To keep it dry,
you told me later –
much later)

At the time it took me by surprise.
I watched the black strands lift clear.
The movement of your fingers –
saw your neck exposed white and bare,
the innocent provocation
of your ear.
I didn't kiss you then,
though you turned
and looked at me as if you thought I might.

But that was the moment
when you stopped and put up your hair;
holding the clips between your teeth so that
your lips drew back,
that I saw a word unspoken,
take shape between our eyes
and hover there.

Shall we go, you said,
I think it's over,
and we began to walk away
as if it were.

But like the midges
that circled at our heads,
the moment
followed after us
through the moist autumn air.

The Gaelic Poets Warned Me

The gaelic poets warned me.
They knew you of old –
your eyes like green stones
on a river bed,
the milk white skin,
the hair raven black
and its sheen.
For centuries they sang
your praise,

but I paid no attention
or had forgotten.
Until I saw you walking naked.
By then it was too late –
my past had caught up with me.
Snared by atavistic beauty,
I fell into history.
All the poems in the English language
will not save me.

The Whiteness of Snow

The whiteness
of snow
on a branch of pine,
is the whiteness
of her skin
from shoulder
to thigh.
And the sway of the branch
under its
flesh of snow,
is the song of her hips
in the weight of my hands.

At Every Window a Different Season

I remember a house
where we sat to watch
the days pass;
hour by hour.
The changing of the light
on mountain and lake.
The year's passage
in an afternoon.
At every window
a different season.

Bog and high grass
climbed the mountains
where sheep lay strewn
like white rocks,
cloud catching in their horns.
There were geese in the boreen,
cows in the hedgerows.
A church spire
and the ocean
at the foot of the garden.

On clear nights
stars shimmered
like cut glass
in the immensity of sky
that wrapped itself
and silence
from end to end of the sleeping fields.

In winter
the roar of wind
drowned speech.
Walls shook and timber.
Wave upon wave
rocked our bed,
a curragh at anchor
on the open sea.

I remember
a half door
thrown wide upon waking.
Hay stacks on the front lawn.
In summer
wild flowers rampant;
iris, primrose, foxglove.
And in the pools of sunshine after rain,
a table and chairs
of wrought iron
set out for late breakfast.

A garden adrift
between mist
and heat haze.
Palm trees,
fuchsia,
mallow.
And the wandering pathways
that led to the sea,
paved by orange flags
we carried stone by stone
from the most westerly strand
in the western world.

A house
full of cats and cooking.
Hanging baskets from the rafters;
plants in the baskets
and cats on the rafters
or sun bathing
under wide-shaded pottery lamps.
A sailor's hammock,
a hearth and crane,
armchairs drawn to the fire.
Coffee on the stove,
wine on the table.
Music at three o'clock in the morning.

I remember a house
where we sat
to watch the days pass
hour by hour.
The changing of the light
over mountain and lake.
The passage of a year
in an afternoon.
At every window
a different season.

The Breath of History

I am not an ordinary woman.
I wake in the morning.
I have food to eat.
No one has come in the night
to steal my child, my lover.
I am not an ordinary woman.

A plum tree
blossoms outside my window,
the roses are heavy with dew.
A blackbird sits on a branch
and sings out her heart.
I am not an ordinary woman.

I live where I want.
I sleep when I'm tired.
I write the words I think.
I can watch the sky
and hear the sea.
I am not an ordinary woman.
No one has offered me life
in exchange for another's.

No one has beaten me until I fall.
No one has burnt my skin
nor poisoned my lungs.
I am not an ordinary woman.
I know where my friends live.
I have books to read,
I was taught to read.
I have clean water to drink.
I know where my lover sleeps;
she lies beside me,
I hear her breathing.
My life is not commonplace.

At night the air
is as sweet as honeysuckle
that grows along the river bank.
The curlew cries
from the marshes
far out,

high and plaintive.
I am no ordinary woman.
Everything I touch and see
is astonishing and rare –
privileged.
Come celebrate each
privileged, exceptional thing:
water, food, sleep –
the absence of pain –
a night without fear –
a morning without
the return of the torturer.

A child safe,
a mother,
a lover, a sister.
Chosen work.
Our lives are not commonplace –
any of us who read this.
But who knows –
tomorrow or the day after …
I feel all about me
the breath of history –
pitiless
and ordinary.

A Woman in Another War

Some days when we kiss
we close our eyes.
Somedays when we close our eyes
we kiss.
Somedays we do not read the newspaper.

A woman was getting on a bus,
I was reading the newspaper.
The woman carried a baby in a carry cot –
Mind your step, another woman said,
and offered her a seat.

I was reading the newspaper –
I was reading the story
of a woman in another country,
a woman in another war.
The story of a woman
who was raped by soldiers.

The soldiers came into her town.
They ordered the women into the street,
they told them to lie on the ground.
They made them lie in rows
and the soldiers raped them
in rows.
One woman after another.
One soldier after another.

One of the women
had a baby,
a newborn baby.
It lay on the earth beside her.
It cried to be fed.
She heard it cry.
She asked the man who was raping her
to stop – to stop
long enough to let her
feed her child.

Bring me my child, she said.
The man stopped.
He got up from her body
and lifted the baby.
He carried it in his arms,
he held it over her.
He took out a knife,
he smiled.
He cut the child's neck from its shoulders
and held the bleeding head
to the woman's breast:
Here's your baby, he said,
feed it.

There was a woman in another country,
a woman in another war.
The soldiers came into the town,
they ordered the women into the streets.
They raped them one after another,
row after row;
one soldier after another,
one woman after another.

The woman on the bus
was helped by another
to sit down.
She lifted the baby
from its cot.
You have to be careful of the head,
the other woman said.
Yes, the woman answered
and with her hand
she cradled the baby's head.

Somedays when we kiss
we close our eyes.
Somedays when we close our eyes
we kiss.
Somedays we don't read the newspaper.

My Grandmother's Voice

Sometimes
when my mother speaks to me
I hear her mother's voice:
my grandmother's
with its trace of Belfast accent
which carried with it
something from every town
the Normans passed through.
My grandmother,
mother of seven,
who will not be quiet yet
twenty years after her death.

Sometimes when I look at my mother
it is her mother I see –
the far sighted gaze,
the way of sitting
bolt upright in a chair –
holding forth, the quick wit,
the fold her hands make in her lap.
The sweep of her hair.

And listening closely
or caught unaware,
I hear my great grandmother
echo between them:
A glance – a tone.
My grandmother's
mother
who died giving birth
to her only child.
Whose words and stories
pent up in her daughter
flowed on
into the talk of my mother.
I catch them now in my own.
My head sings with their conversation.

And hearing them –
this fertile
and ghostly orchestration –

I am sorry to have brought them
to the end of their line.
Stopped them in their track
across millennia.
From what primeval starting point
to here?
A relay race
through centuries
from mother to daughter –
an expression passed on
a gesture,
a profile.

Their voices reverberate in my head.
They will die with me.
I have put an end to inheritance –
drawn a stroke across the page.
Their grace,
their humour,
their way of walking in a room.
The stoicism
that carried them all this way
has stopped with me;
the first of their kind
who will not bear their gift
and burden.

I lift my pen
quickly, wanting
to set down all the stories
spoken by these busy, eloquent,
long lived women
who never had a moment
to sit down
or lift a pen.

I begin.
A young woman, a protestant
from Belfast,
married a sea captain,
a catholic
who drowned at sea ...

from
Like Joy in Season,
Like Sorrow
(2001)

Uncharted Passage

You are the flagship —
gladly or not
we travel in your wake.

So long as the masthead
bears your colours
we hold course.

Though you founder,
almost, in this
uncharted passage

Where storm and shallows
threaten alike. Though
we stand-to helpless

While half a lifetime's
cargo is jettisoned
and the flotsam

Of memory; the silks
and the bric-a-brac,
float out,

On an ebb tide. Yet,
so long as you endure
we are young.

So long as you hoard
a remnant of self
above water,

A frail bulwark
survives.
In shared middle-age

We remain, all
of us — somebody's
children, still.

Each Day Our First Night

What a beautiful mother
I had —
Forty years ago,
When I was young
And in need of a mother.
Tall and graceful,

Dark haired,
Laughing.
What a fine mother, I had
When I was young.
Now I climb the steps
To a cold house

And call out a word
That used to summon her.
An old woman
Comes to the door:
Gaunt eyed, grey haired,
Feeble. An old woman

Who might be
Anybody's mother. She
Fumbles with the locks,
And smiles a greeting
As if the name spoken
Belonged to her.

We go inside
And I make tea.
The routine questions
Used to prompt her
Fall idle.
She cannot remember

The day of the week,
The hour, nor
The time of year.
Look at the grass,
I say,
Look at the leaves –

You tell me!
Autumn, she answers
At last. Her hands
Wind in her lap,
Her eyes like a child's,
Full of shame.

Each day,
A little more
Is lost of her.
Captured for an instant,
Then gone.
Everything that

Made her particular,
Withering, like leaf
From the tree.
Her love of stories
And song, her wit,
The flesh on her bones.

What a beautiful mother
I had, forty years ago
When I was young
And in need of a mother.
Proud, dark haired
Laughing.

Now I descend the path
From a cold house,
An old woman
Follows to the window,
An old woman
Who might be

Anybody's mother.
She stands patiently
To wave me off –
Remembering
The stage directions,
Of lifted hand

And longing gaze.
In this
Experimental piece –
Each day,
Our first night –
She plays her part

With such command –
Watching her
Take a last bow
From the curtain –
You could swear she
Was born for it!

Grist to the Mill

All grist to the mill,
You say, or at least,
That's how I console
Myself, for wasting so
Much of your precious
Time. I have to remind
My brain, consciously –
That a writer can make
Use of everything.

I sit on the edge
Of the hospital bed,
Lifting the spoon
To your mouth.
Nothing is wasted,
You say,
No experience,
However dismal –
Entirely redundant.
I wipe your chin
With the napkin
Isn't that true?
You ask me,
Wanting it to be.

And thus you offer –
And I resolve
To make it so –
To take this sorrow –
This irreparable loss;
The erasure
By stealth,
Of culture and past –
This commonplace and
Unreported suffering,
And put them to work.

To take your humour,
Your bafflement, the
Sudden shafts of vision,
Your dark ironies –
And shape them –
Honing them
Into an artifact –
Something
One can take up
And put down.
Something that
Can be looked at
And looked away from.

Unlike this –
This sly dispossession –
This infant dependence
And fear, which
Even your gallows humour,
And that
Family heirloom –
Pride,
Will not mask.
And which once seen
I cannot unsee.

And so I determine
To use them – the
Damage and indignities,
Piled day by day, onto
The wreckage of self.
To put them to service –
Like a scrap and bone
Monger –
Grist to the mill.
For your sake –
For mine.

The Poet and Satire

'What is this life so full of care
We have no time to stand and stare.
No time to stand beneath the boughs
And stare as long as sheep or cows.'

You are eating lunch at the kitchen
Table. I am washing the dishes.
You are gazing into the garden,
There's something familiar

About that garden, you say,
Holding your fork in the air
Forgetting to eat. There certainly
Ought to be – you've been looking

At it for sixty years, I reply.
I am washing dishes at the kitchen
Sink. You are holding your fork
In the air, neglecting to eat.

Have I? you ask, sceptical,
But not enough to argue the point.
Isn't it an amazing thing –
Memory, the tricks it plays.

Why should I remember that
Poem after all these years
And forget so much else?
I am washing dishes at the

Kitchen sink. You are playing
With lunch at the kitchen table,
Too thoughtful to eat. It would be
A wonderfully interesting study,

My condition, you say, if I
Could stand back and observe it.
Finish your dinner before it's
Cold, I answer. I am washing

Dishes at the kitchen sink.
I always thought it was
A satiric poem, you say. Would
You call it a satiric poem?

The poet must be laughing
At himself, surely, to write
'And stare as long as sheep
Or cows?' I am washing dishes

At the kitchen sink. Who cares
What kind of poem it is, I think.
I have the housework to do.
Look at the lovely white

Rose by the fence, you say,
The last rose of summer!
I am washing dishes at the
Kitchen sink. I do not care

About satire or roses. Have
You finished your broccoli?
I ask. You are gazing into
The autumn garden (something

Familiar about it, you know)
Who would guess, you
Remark, after a moment's pause,
That you were the well known poet –

I say – look at the glorious
Rose – the last of summer.
And what do you say? Have you
Finished your broccoli!

Frost

And here you are now,
on the threshold –
half a ghost
already.
In the long corridors
of your mind
you pace,
haunting yourself.

Your eyes gaze out
from uncurtained
windows.
Damp has risen
through the bare boards
and seeped into
your voice.

And look –
along the pathway
that led to the sea –
on the grass
and on the hedges,
a first frost has formed.
It glitters on
your hair
and skin.

These Days of Languor

These days of languor –
loosed of everything
but pleasure
and time.

Enthral to sense,
we put on clothes
only at late evening.
One moment

leading to the next
and back again.
At last,
light fading

on the balcony,
we spread a cloth
and eat –
oysters,

avocado,
new strawberries.
In candle flame, as
you lift your glass

I see love's stain –
wine red
under your
fingernails.

The Rapture of Senses

Love –
is not only
the love of the body –
the rapture of senses.
It is also

Work,
and forbearance.
Hoping
against hope.
Turning a blind eye,

Holding the tongue.
Speaking out
when it's dangerous.
It is impetuous,
foolish,

Quick witted,
incautious,
letting the heart
rule the head.
It is forgetting

Offense,
forgoing dignity.
Falling out,
reconciling.
It is being alike

And being various,
agreeing
to disagree,
or taking the trouble
to fight.

It is thinking
the same thought
in different places.
Or in the one place,
looking silently

In contrary directions.
It is cooking
for two, at evening
when only one
is hungry.

Or wakeful in the
small hours,
quiet, while
the other sleeps.
It is laughing aloud

For no reason.
Weeping
in secret,
for the others
grief.

Love —
is not only
the love of the body —
the rapture of senses.
But if it were this

And nothing more —
it would be love
enough —
my love,
for one lifetime.

Keeping Vigil

It is not that the world
Is safer —
Wars ravage as usual. Children
Die unnoticed, in our sleep.
Along the same fragrant roads,
Between the olive groves
And that gilded sea —
Where we first embraced —
Women are herded to slaughter.

It is not that the sky
Shelters us,
From loss or betrayal
Or prophecies of storm.
It is not that the days
Are longer, or that the
Stars can pierce
The sulphurous city nights.

It is not that our lives
Are easy —
Our best work thwarted
Our language scarred —
It is not that comforts
Make comfortable,
That love endures,
Or that any of us
Will escape our fate —
These tracks of iron
Laid on sleepers, run
In one direction only.

It is not the moments
Of epiphany — the unlooked
For transfigurations
Of the earthly — such as,
On a frozen field
Where we stopped to kiss —

Emerging from a snow-bound
Wood, a herd of deer –
Suddenly –
Their antlers blown like
Driftwood on a white lake.

It is not that the world
Is better – (beyond the
Perimeter wire, you too,
Hear the cries that fret
The edge of silence.)
It is only that you kept
Vigil, with me, here,
On this station platform,
Waiting for change,
Or for light. That hour
After hour you stared
Into the blizzard mouth –
Watching for a sign of thaw.

It is not that the world
Is safer –
Yet, in darkness, you fall
Asleep at my side, and when
You wake, the day opens with
You; startled, mercurial –
Like a first morning,
Making breakfast or love.
Quick to merriment,
To argument and surprise.
It is not that the world
Is safer. Only this –
That I love your gaiety.

Time Has Made a Mirror

Sometimes,
I stretch my hands
to the light.
Wanting
to see you again.

Time has made them
a mirror.
It seems
in your absence,
they have grown

To resemble yours –
taken your shape,
your attitudes.
Or is it,
only,

The wide bands
of silver
that I wear now
on the third finger
of each hand

That gives them
this air
of reflecting yours?
Is it time?
Or these pieces

Of silver
that has made them
a mirror –
of your strength?
Your suffering?

In Your Shoes

When you were gone
I found a pair of shoes

you had left behind
under the bed.

I put them on, wanting
to know how they felt.

The leather was worn
and intimate,

loose across the instep.
I walked to the window

and then to the door.
My heel slipped free

but the toes pinched.
I wanted to see how

it felt in your shoes —
constrained or easy.

I wanted to see
how it felt to be you —

when you wore them and
walked free of me.

Endless Days

I miss
the endless days –
emptying
one
into the other.
Piling up at the window
like rain.
Or snow.

I miss
the hills
flushed
crimson at evening –
and at day break
clouds stalking
the drenched fields.

I miss
the quarrels
and the laughter.
The stillness.
A favourite chair
by the fire.

I miss
the sight of you –
your eyes,
your hands,
your knees.
The sight of you.

I miss
the endless days
emptying
one into another.
Time
piling up at the window
like snow.

And now,
in a foreign street
when rain begins
and someone says –
Let's make for home,
I miss a house
I turn towards still.

from
Perhaps the Heart is Constant After All
(2012)

Perhaps the Heart is Constant after All

Perhaps the heart is constant after all. Perhaps it
makes no difference who we love, what voice lures
us, what name we call. It's always the same love is
it not? Drawn from the one spring, coursing the same

Track. It's always the same thirst we slake, the
same image in the pool; the same blood dimmed gaze.
Perhaps it makes no difference who we lust for –
isn't it always the same veil we cast over each new

Form; the finest gossamer illusion can buy, spun
from the sheerest silks of faith, hope and deceit?
What can it signify at the end of it whose gaze
ensnares? Isn't it always the same sirenian song,

The same wine on the tongue, the same salt in the
wound? If the heart is faithful in the least, is it to
the elemental, the universal theme? Is it only in
particulars that love betrays – the setting and the

Costumes: a certain sky, a certain street, oleander
at an open gate, a spiral stairs, a white coverlet –
the weather and the houses, the language and the
streets: surface things, easily exchanged, forgotten

Shed like leaves or skin, like memory itself. Like
the imprint of sight and touch: breath on glass, a
particular face. Perhaps, this too at last will wane,
and with it the afterglow: a certain night, a scented

Road, the scarred river, the lamp-lit bridge: a lover
crossing over; crossing back – a stranger. Even this,
too at last will fade, erased like time itself. Like the
memory of her face. Like the memory of that lie.

Blood

Her glance strays from yours –
her ears quicken to
another voice.
Turn from her –
say nothing.
At night your blood
feeds the white page.

The Grace of the Given

If you should wake one morning to find it come again –
languishing at your doorstep naked, seductive, do not
seek to know its genesis, its cause or destination. Do
not ask if the arrival is timely or fitting. If you should
wake from dream to find it come again – startled and
sensuous at your table, forsake all thought of purpose,

Of benefit or cost – especially, do not repent the
days consumed by arduous sloth waiting for the word,
nor yet the profligate nights spent feasting your gaze
on the one chosen form. In these two, the journey is
all. In poetry as in love – this imperative alone to heed:
surrender to the grace of the given: toil for it, praise it.

Sweet Fool Beware

Moon –
the blue silk of your glance
enthralls mine, flung upon slate
like a shawl. Its chill glamour drifts
magisterial, sequins the square
between my roof and hers. Its

Bone –
china touch strays to my window,
fingers the glass of my dreams. Come
hither, come hither sweet fool, it schemes,
and dance to my lunatic, ruinous tune –
and dance to my ruinous, lunatic tune.

Summer

I want to be walking down an avenue in summer, my arm
about my beloved. I want the avenue tree-lined, my hand
along your waist, the boughs above our heads arched, the
filigree of leaves reflected, the brindled light throwing open
the path before us. The lake will be misted in the still torpor

Of late afternoon. I want the birds to be singing – so many
we cannot count or name them. I want to lean against you,
as you do in summer, walking down an avenue. I want to
whisper in your ear: I want you, as you do in such weather,
nonchalant, not needing an answer, my arm about your waist

As you lean into me, the warm flesh of your back beneath
its fine cotton, damp under my hand as we walk down a tree-
lined avenue; careless, in summer heat of love, careless with
youthful negligence of happiness. I want it to be summer again.
I want my senses to be blithe and greedy, as in youth before

Everything happened. I want to be walking down a tree-lined
avenue, the branches casting their slumberous shadow, the air
dense with the scent of evening languor as we saunter: my arm
around your waist, through the corridor of dark leaf, sunlight
beckoning at its mouth – as we walk from winter into summer.

Stilling Sense

The last sunlight of the year, amber and violet tinted
will fall across the slate-grey waters of the bay. You will
stand silent. Your mind will empty. In a slow, loosening swell,
the sea will unroll itself, dense and oiled. As the wave runs
in, the tolling of a bell, resonates, as it breaks on the black
slab of a granite pier. As the wind blows through it. As it
whitens the air; rising. You will stand silent. Your mind will
empty. It will wash away from you then, time present and
time past. All of it. You will stay or you will not. As the sea
rolls in. As the breaking wave whitens the air and falls. As
it sucks through sand and shingle –
as it eddies and retreats.

You will stand at the edge of the world in silence where
the waves break on a stone shore. The shore that is gouged
by the sea, enveloped, beaten and sheltered. The skies will
brighten or fade. Your mind will empty. You will choose. Or
you will not. The sea will be turquoise and azure and purple
becoming. It will turn, reform and again advance. Each break,
each dissolution, finding its end in its beginning. Your mind
will empty. You will stay or not. Each forfeiture, white and
sibilant, a new place starting. It will all be behind you then,
the place and the time, even the names dissolving. Your mind
will empty. The skies will be carmine and gold and back again.
You will stand on the shore in silence. The last sunlight of the
year will fall across slate-blue water –
somewhere a bell tolling...

Alien Familiar

Never before at close quarters, more curious
than shy, as dawn broke on the rough forest
track, a young badger ambled into my path, its
wide, brindled back smoothing the bracken,
the soft hips swaying, hands and feet muffled
in its mythic overcoat and between the
teeth, an early breakfast – a red and yellow
apple gripped. At the sight of me, it stopped to
gape. No fear in its face only puzzlement, the
broad spade of the muzzle stretched towards
me, nostrils black and flaring. Rooted

To ground by a chance encounter in a clearing
of oak – fixedly staring at the wonder of other:
this alien familiar, the intimate detail of form
and regalia, did either sense in the half-light, the
camouflage of intention? A snare laid before
memory, its trail concealed at our first step? We
stood still for how many moments more? I bowed
my head in homage. The badger held my gaze –
then slowly blinked. With this formality we parted.
It ploughed its lazy, shuffling route deeper into
shelter. I went the opposite way towards light.

Lee Shore

Storm in spring
astonishes the lake –
the sky is ruptured,
the rain capsized.

A north wind, exultant
dredges the air –
hauls the birch tree
weeping to ground.

Distant, on the lee shore
among reeds at anchor –
four white swans
breast the white wave.

Odysseys of Light

December night shepherds its sky —
eternity strewn wide across the heavens.
Incalculable nativities, odysseys of light:
fathomless as the silence or its memory.

Far out, the dead gaze down, their pale eyes
glimmering, supplicant; inarticulate as stars.
Below, earthbound we gather winter fuel,
yearning, like our breath is fringed with ice.

Aolean Song

1.

In a field by the river the swan has left her wings behind. Side by
side, the two white shells, like twin harps, stirred by the wind, stand
upright at the centre of the sheep-shorn grass. They might be the
sails of a child's boat forgotten in the morning mist or the cloth
wings of a dancer shrugged off carelessly at front of stage. You could
imagine a dress rehearsal; you could fancy she had merely slipped
out for an unexpected costume change and that at any moment she
will reappear to loud applause. You can picture her return: how she
might lift the ribbed fabric to her shoulders and standing poised
at the water's edge, launch her beauty one more time into the
empty sky. The air beaten to fine silver by the thunder of her flight.

2.

The fox must have come at dawn, or minutes before, the mist not
yet risen from the field, the air heavy with its chill, shrouding the
bank where ducks and geese were sound asleep, heads shoveled
down deep into sleek tail feathers. No one would have glimpsed
him nor heard his tread. He must have crept to the water's edge:
the lean torso brushing the meadow, the empty stomach drawn
tight as a drum, the fiery standard borne low and motionless.
The herons concealed in the rushes would have been the first to
wake, their hearts run through seconds before the terrible cry
reached their ears – that first savage snatch as the jaws closed
round the throat, as the head was forced below water, would have
roused the lake. The fox must have tightened his grip then and
heaved the struggling body over the dew-laden pasture, the
awkward limbs tangling with his own. He would have sunk his teeth
into the warm, palpitating flesh, the blood spouting, his flared

3.

Nostrils flooded and the russet chest. You could be glad almost for
the fox having such a feast, alfresco, in the first fine weather
of the year. You might be glad that his belly was full for once, that
for one day at least he could rest from his gruesome profession –
the family trade of predation. This is how it must have happened.
You can think of no other explanation that fits the facts. Or the lack
of them – the pallid wings posed unsullied on the ground, the delicate
ribcage flawless. No trace of blood – no stain, no stench. The soft
bruised offal, all eaten up warm, the whole mossy plate licked clean.

4.

This immaculate scene might tempt you to conceive of something
mystical: you could fancy that the swan had merely wearied of
these appendages, had wanted all at once, to be free of their
demand to achieve the inconceivable with every beating of her limbs.
And that, like a dancer at the final curtain call, on an impulse
she had rid herself of their weight, wanting to be ordinary perhaps –
commonplace for an hour, to escape her destiny: the day after
day tireless reinvention of the miraculous. You might well

5.

Invoke this theory or some other soft deception, unable to bear
the resonance of that horrific shriek – upon the first incision
and the second – the tearing of the gullet, the belly ripped
asunder, the gleaming guts spilled out onto the verdant plain,
greedily devoured while she watched, from one wild eye, her
own consumption. You might prefer to imagine almost any other
telling of the story. You might cling to the consolation of fable –

6.

A magical inversion of the legendary. Could some super-normal power, some mystic intercession have spared her on the brink of death? Might she have like Etain – the most beautiful woman in Ireland – been stolen away by the Sídhe and changed by them into human form? Enchanted by their song could she have fled this earth and all its sorrows on the snow-white feet of a girl? The seductive urging of fairy tale, the redemptive force of myth. You might easily imagine this.

7.

Daylight would have gaped and stretched its glare all the way across the lake by the time the fox was fully finished breakfast. He would most probably have taken time to savour it. No way of knowing how long he could have waited for exactly this. He might have come to the same spot every night for a week or more; lying alone in the chill of damp fern. He might have gone away more ravenous than he arrived. You could be relieved that on this one startling morning his luck was in. By the time he was quite ready other creatures would be up and busy about the business of the day. He would, more than likely, have hauled the

8.

Carcass further inland to polish off the last remains at leisure. He would not have stopped to clean himself until almost home. There must have been feathers clinging at his lips as he strolled along, blood on his long, grey muzzle, on his glistening breast. His jaw must have ached a little from the effort, his heavy legs moved more slowly. He might have wished as he crossed back through the forest that he had not quite so far to go. He might have wished that just this once, he had wings to fly.

Artist at Life

Your presence adorns
the morning. A still life
escapes its frame as you
speak. On white linen

You paint new apples;
their ripening and blush,
black grapes for your eyes
imitate, and the greenest

Of green olives their line.
At the rim of the glass,
red wine with its lustre
stains the cloth and your

Mouth. For background,
rose petals, faded, are
strewn on a floor where a
soft breasted hunting dog

Waits at command. The
burnish of oil for the voice,
the finest brush stroke
draws the brow. Flesh as

Canvas; maker or made. With
a touch of the hand, swallows
flock at a window. Ochre –
the colour of their flight.

A Disposition Inherited

At a dressing table mirror a woman regards her image.
She is studying the scorch lines of a sorrow that has
since early morning, seized possession of her life. She
draws herself to full height, tilts the glass and with
ancient skill, as if it were a newly purchased hat or silk
stole she is fitting about her shoulders, adjusts her gaze

And composes her reflection. She must judge how best
to wear the wound when she walks before the world.
Her hand for an instant flies to her throat where the
blood beats up. She trembles at the unexpected force,
this grief still caustic that brands her flesh as it makes
passage into the commonplace. For already she knows it

Has come to stay. She remembers how it will settle,
the stealth of it: in her veins like sand, between her
bones – shrapnel. She gathers a fistful of hair; winds it
about her neck as if she might resist an unwanted familiar
that will wake her each morning, sleep with her at night,
greet her from this on, at every door she enters. She

Steadies her hands, gathers resolve. So that its pressure
will bear less on others, she must choose where to store the
loss. She will mould it into a way of being: an attribute
so constant even her children will forget to sense it. And
in time will walk free of her, impatient for their share of
carelessness. Seeing her resolute step and lifted brow

People will agree that she always had the knack of
carrying trouble lightly. Only friends will recognise its
origin: a disposition inherited – from her mother's side,
they'll say. An attitude of mind or spirit – old fashioned.
What used they call it – that valiant air, in her day?
Was it grace under fire; men at war, liked to praise?

To Lengthen Our Days

From your new listening post: a reserved suite in
the ante-room, you watch over us still, alert to
error and exaggeration. You hear us before we

Speak. See us before we appear. Stripped to
bone, immobile; distilled it seems to a symbol of
yourself, a graven image on a wall, an effigy

Of motherhood. 'Cease thou thy worrying,' you
council when you see my worried face. 'There's
nothing that requires concern. I'm perfectly well,'

You state. 'And after all what can we do? Dust
to dust. Each of us must die of something.' 'How
do you manage it?' I ask. 'What?' you say. 'Finding

Reasons: keeping on, keeping on? Because all things
considered, it's what I know best,' you say. 'A cog
in the wheel?' I suggest. 'No – a link in the chain.'

Fledgling

How proud I was –
how well you did it.
Staunch as a soldier
on parade.
No rehearsal –
first time off.
All new to us both.
Your old body
white sheathed
on the bed,
eyes shut,
mouth wide, your
tongue like a
fledging's furled.
A small bird
testing the air for
a morsel of death.

Soul's Flight

How easily your soul escaped its body –
the instant your heart stopped –
lithe as a dancer –
it stepped out,
a young woman again,
stretching bare limbs to the sun,
tossing back her chestnut
hair, on the first fine morning of summer.

The shroud of wax cast off, a flowered,
sleeveless frock put on, for shade
a wide brimmed hat –
setting off early to bathe new
sense and all along the track –
the perfume of yellow gorse in bloom.

How lightly your soul stepped out.

But when a year before, the warrant
served, they came to take your
body from its house, they
wrenched it by the root.
Coffined on a stretcher,
they hauled you down, your fingers
bleeding on the newel-post, your eyes
beseeching the light to yield one last glimpse.

The flesh yet warm, the undertakers
claimed their part, the
bits and useless treasures –
pictures, books and crockery,
followed down the garden
path, born aloft in funeral
procession, the flotsam of a life:
a walnut table, a writing desk,
the Boston rocker your mother gave you.

When they took your body from its house
they had to tear it by the root. The
grave diggers, its ultimate
companions, assumed their station,
with practiced stride while hymns
were sung and gods praised,
they shoveled in the clay, silt
rising on the floorboards, stifling memory.

Blinding the windows that looked to eternity,
that had stood to watch with you
each change of tide and the
hourly parade of worlds.
One task remained before the final
sod was turned: they gathered sand
and stone and muzzled the chimneys
that listened constant still –
to the day-breaking choir
and the evening valedictory of the gulls.

But how easily your soul escaped its body.
The instant your heart stopped,
astonished by grace,
a young girl stepped out –
lissom as an athlete,
eager, stretching smooth limbs
to the sun, tossing out her gilded hair.
All about her the revelry of a crowded beach.

The excited cry of swimmers – tumbling
in the silken waves, arms
raised at her advance –
beckoning, calling her in
to bathe new sense;
their voices buoyed by history,
where cliff meets sky.
In the dazzled flux
their haloed image her guide.
Yellow gorse scenting the
air, on the first clear morning of spring.

Writer at Work

Beginning once more after long absence, you have
forgotten all of it; even the common rituals of
evocation. How to listen, how to idle, how in
darkness to strike a bargain with the dead. So
you rehearse in order, ancient rites of passage
to still sense, make welcome. First light the lamp,

Set a fire for heat. As in an old, disused house, to
air the soul; throw all the windows wide. Then,
silence laid, and white page, words in vigil, sit and
let the ghosts come in. Gingerly at first, fleeting,
from the corner of an eye, a glimpse is caught or
scent, a sudden breeze, casts a footstep on the

Stairs, a tremor or a sigh. Flame drifts on glass.
Slowly they gain force, the shadows murmurous.
Every voice is known to you, each breath resonant.
Only you have altered after all. They take their places
one by one, the last to leave is the first returned.
Each draws another under the lintel, a necklace of

Pearl, strung in the order of their loss. Do not question,
nor reproach as they congregate. Accept the only
consolation they can offer; their memories of you,
invulnerable to time. Take what you can see and hear,
abandon touch, breath on skin. No power of longing
can restore this earthly gift. Do not be afraid then –

Stay; let them cluster at the hearth, about your table.
Grave or whimsical, out of their element, do not ask of
them what they did not ask to lose: weight, coherence.
Sit, hear them out. They have come all this way only to
render an account. As the light grows cold, stay. Do not
turn your back on their entreaty; their clamorous hunger.

New Poems

Lover

You follow me in dream. Only in dream.

From hearth to hearth, your shadow
at each door comes knocking. A face
flickers white at the pane, your step soft
on the stairs. In my mother's kitchen,
at dusk you came seeking, to know from
her, long dead; if she had glimpsed
me, here or there, in half-light or in dark.

You follow me in dream. Only in dream.

Through dinner table clamour, at the
house of my friends, I hear your voice
insistent, enquiring after me, the why
and how of it. Supplicant from room to
room, amid guests discarded, idle chairs.

You follow me in dream. Only in dream.

Huge in wonder, your eye's gaze untainted,
at times a child's grace comes looking. At
others, a spoiled cheek is turned, cruelty
sparkles on your tongue, with the avarice
for wounds, of those grown up in hurting.

You follow me in dream. Only in dream.

I feel on the air between us your ringed
fingers softly sifting through indexed notes
on leaves of vellum. As you gather and
annotate, while you prepare impromptu
seminars from hand-stitched manuscripts –
on love abandoned, and loss mislaid.

You follow me in dream. Only in dream.

Your infant soul, insomniac, seeks my
name from street to street, in antique
quest, among the newly found, the recently
forgot. There and here, amid the dead
and the living, a face at the pane, in my
mother's house, your step soft on the stairs.

You follow me in dreams. Only in dreams.

In Praise of Small Things

It's not in everyone's house –
that I would lift an apple
from the plate
before my coat is off –
and eat it without asking.
Only under
an old friend's roof,
or lover's,
would I have felt such
license,
welcome stacked
like fuel at a hearth,
like the years unnoticed.

Or at my mother's table
tea drawn
bread rising
where everything hers
waited to be shared.
And the meeting of minds
was all that she counted.
So find a compliment
in rude disguise,
the way I help myself
in your kitchen –
before invitation.

Planning and Calculus

My father was a careful man, a learned man. A mathematician who loved literature, music and wild countryside. A foresighted man, he took stock of circumstances and made his decisions based on logic and reason. An actuary whose job it was to calculate risk

to assess the probability of anything happening to anyone at any given moment. The likelihood of benefit and loss. The cost. This, his professional task at which he was both skilled and practiced. My father died when I was seven years of age. He left behind

a wife and five young children. To fend unaided. At times of dire necessity when all plans and effort failed her, his widow used to smile and say, 'Think of Mr. Macawber, something will turn up.' At times worse still, on desperation's brink, she would

declare, 'Well, we'll have to ask Eilish,' her dead sister, 'to intercede for us.' My mother had stamina, intelligence and fortitude. She outlived her husband by fifty-six years. When she was ninety-three and I half that, on the doorstep of

death she was still making light of things, 'Oh, something will turn up,' she said to raise a laugh with nearly the end of her breath. From these threads and swatches of shared histories, did I learn to put faith less in prognosis and fine calculation

than in those disruptions of narrative that pitch us from comfort and clarity? Keeping one foot in the door that opens onto providence, was this the lesson passed down through her line? And she would say if she could hear me, as she often

said, listening to me embark on some high-flown notion, 'Now don't be sententious please. There's nothing at all unusual about me.' And I would tease and carry on regardless happy to provoke her as I often was and am still. Should I have questioned then

had I been able, had there been space as she lay at the graves
open pit making last jokes, to make the last easy; do you think,

that we stumble into harmony with divine intent, should I have
asked, only when we abandon will and self? Might surrender to

chance, a lust for senselessness, for the sweet, sheer hell of it
all – be the principle that inspires our breath, that orchestrates
each living pulse that beats in time with happenstance? And she
would answer were she able, 'Oh that's much too deep for this

small head. I'll have to think about it all when I go to bed tonight.'

Damage

She warned you at the start. Once. You would

acknowledge that. 'I will disappoint,' she said.
'I will not be enough. My sins are always those
of omission. Silent.' You heard the syllables like
warm stones cast into a pool, hissing drop by
drop. 'I parch the things I love.' But the month
was August, the air perfumed, sultry. We crossed
the stream, picked watercress, forget-me-nots,
along its brimming edge, wild mint. Drank wine
in yellow fields under the loose, stacked hay.
What could your senses comprehend of lack? A
heart still born? How to recognise stigmata in the
bloom of love-struck skin? She warned you at the
start. You had to give her that. But the month was
August. The weather hot. Your eyes were tuned
to meadowsweet, thriving on a riverbank –
honeysuckle, cattle on a hillside drowsing. A sky
of gentian. And swifts caroling exultant as flight –

high as the clouds. If there had been clouds.

Patchwork

1.

From where does the love
of poetry,
the reading and the making
of it stem? What impulse brings
us back to it, from the city
from the cloud, on our knees
from grief and joy and strife?
Is it the last refuge
of the romantic, fervent or
disenchanted? Is it the craving
for order in a disordered world?
Is it a coverlet, a patchwork
stitched in seclusion
from scraps and remnants,
the off-cuts that fall from the
passage of the day
from faith, fear and passion?

2

Is it to run a needle through flesh –
through one's own flesh –
drawing the fine thread from
the eye, to the lips
to the hands, to the stomach,
to the heart?
Making from the quick of life
a woven cloth, a vivid tapestry
to hang on a wall;
its script open to the world
as if to say here it is –
this is the blood,
the beating pulse, the joy,
the wonder, the grief,
this is what it cost.
This is what I made of it.

The Big House

The house waits: those dispersed, departed spirits will return –
will fill the halls again. The call is irresistible. The house is patient,
its memory long.
Like a bird in flight, reflected in its glowing crystal, light dashes
trembling from pane to window. The burnished gusts, murmurous
in autumn that
billow softly through high chimneys, in winter turn to tempest raw
and rail at bolt and slate as if some grief long unassuaged begs
harbour from its haunting.

When spring announces general change, the shift of key and shade
has tipsy fieldmice run abroad in gossamer-costumed air, cats
cavort among the heather-bells
while cows sing in clover. Woken early, majestic boughs, oak and
ash lower their listening heads, by the clock tower the hare halts
ears en pointe,
cooks gossip in the laundry, among the laurels gardeners brood,
scribes and swallows in their lofty roosts dispute, each busy at their
own meticulous craftings.

Before it, mortal and mortar in the sweep of august fantasy slip the
noose of definition, the sultry noon day sun maddens lake and pasture,
its silken glisten
inverting the skies, a brimming mirror of waters full with varicoloured
swift sails and blowsy cumulus. Low and high, past count of hours,
flowers flirtatious and painters
merge, bees and poets drowse and discourse in their tousled beds, limbs
laden with soused anticipation: the perfumed offerings of the flesh, the
spiced gifts of table.
By afternoon while interrogative rooks survey the lie of land, the
goshawk's pinnacle-eye scrutinises earthly strivings, the many puttings-
off and shy
participations, the quickset flamings, soft gutterings in passageway and
drawing room, all are noted and remarked in gilded oils or slow calligraphy
for those who follow later
or in rude advance of expectation. Out wild, along the blossoming avenue,
that leads

serpentine to woods and gate lodge where names are murmured yet
between the hedgerows, amid the bustle of hydrangea, the herons shriek,
the fox sagacious,
ambling contented from the Sunday hunt. Here, where the voices come
and go without their faces, the names of those who came and stayed,
those returned or those
who did not show, are unforgotten, all those who can not now or ever
come, whispered in memorial by geese-white lough and leaf-strewn rain.
But the great interior

knows more than all, its stone and timber, walls and rafters store the
ineluctable. It attends through drought and storm. It promises or persuades
that intention
outlasts matter. Nothing expressed is lost, nothing given form will vanish.
In its opulent, peopled slumber it saves beneath a steepled roof the harvest,
an inventory of
the profane and sacramental, the sequestered imaginings of all those who
cultivate icons of refuge and redemption, those who in sleep break bread still

at its board. All those it has foreseen, summoned and dreamed into breath.

Preliterate

You wanted to go down in flames, you said. One last triumphal
fever. Who cared if wing and bone in the final fury of departure,
were turned to ash and cinder? He understood, your good
friend said, he knew how very much you shared. So deep with
both of you, I see, the love of arts and learning. 'How you must
dream,' he said, 'of conversations on a theme, by a quiet hearth
at evening.' The look he cast held reverence and not a little envy.

'But who gives a toss?' you rudely scorned, 'for tropes and plots,
analysis or parsing? That never once was something I
was after.' His bright face dimmed, 'But I thought you liked to
feel how much it mattered that she loved to read,' he asked
perplexed, 'that literature played for her a vital part?' You stared
at him askance. 'Just knowing that it did, is what I meant, just
knowing that we might some day, some lazy languid afternoon lie

flank by flank and read a book – the thought of that as background
would sweeten every thrust – the life of mind forgotten would set
our breath alight. Then, would I have us both preliterate, ignorant
and mute. The cold sheets burning at our touch, the air might
fume in time with each wrung cry and all around us, books: poetry
immortal and novels, stacked in pyramid at our head, history
in volume, like laurel at our feet, laid slumbering, still and shut.'

Arabesque

And for me, without choice, constructed as I am
by nature and culture, with a flowering of words
metaphoric, allegorical, forever on the tip of an
alliterative tongue, and she, born as she was in

the city of Venice: a storm of caresses, careless
evocative, primed at the brim of her fingers – how
could either one of we two hope to decipher the
native charts of the other or find our way straight

along this twice forked tongue? From the outset
programmed, are we, to false starts, wrong turns,
pathways delusionary through the maze, in this
twinned language of ours, each in its own way

prone to excess, to sport and to play, to intended
prevarication, seductions instinctive which by
times could draw us to a confluence inspired, at
others, conviction too certain for clarity? For do

we tempt, when we exercise these graces inbred, our
own minds astray? As when I speak, as though from
the heart, can even I know if the satinate phrases
that slip express or create it? Do I confess myself

in my talk or coerce imagination through speech?
And she? Oh, she with the virtuosity of birthplace:
an orchestra of gesture unrivalled, are her secrets
revealed in the body's eloquent arabesque or composed

there? Does the fragrance of symbol inebriate reason
as suave sentences do? Or could it be that truth is made
pure for her also in that pause, luminous, carnal when
affect reaches out to touch skin and thought shapes? Ah,

but take heed, reflect – is one of these two crafted, a
director's cut – a story older by far than this – a novel
enactment of a primal theme? So ask her then if she
knows, as no one but she is able, do her hands uncover

sense in this art only – the teasing of blood into heat?

Heat

All day –
in heat
beat   beat   beating –
the cicadas
all morning in heat –
without thought –
chant   chant   chanting.

Without pity –
all day singing,
in heat throbbing –
their cymbals
open and
closing –
singing   singing   singing –
they beat
beat   beat   beat.

Afternoon –
shutters drawn
between sheets
you sprawl   humid –
too hot to stir
your brain in fever
your thoughts
of her.

In the blood
like crickets
throb
throbbing –
in leaves covered
beating
merciless
in heat

through brain
pulsing –

uncovered
your dreams
unstopping –
of her –
beat   beat   and beat   beating
your dreams unstopping
of her –
beat   beat   and beat.

Midwinter

The dark nights claim our days, the battery of wind,
the groaning sea, hail stoning our sight. The dark nights
    claim our days. Waking again at four, mourning the
refusal of light. Waking again, to hear my voice calling
your name aloud. As though you might answer. The
    dark of night claims our days. How long can it be
since your name ringing out in darkness, twenty years
or more, brought you back? How long since you
    answered? How long since, hearing this one cry you
turned? Now your naked back retreating is offered
alone to the camera. You cross a courtyard unseeing,
    gale-blown sleet blinding the ground, untouchable.
Too late for changing. Only in nightmare can there
now arrive this dreamed of reversal of time. Our days
    are eaten by night, waking to darkness again.
Sleeping into darkness again, waking yet again to
another refusal of light. Bound soul and flesh in the
    swaddling garments of night. As if never again can

it break, the brilliance of a sky violet or golden,
breaching the weight of the earth on our faces. And
    yet, yesterday, yes, at the laboured birth of the
shortest day, beneath the great oak at the edge of the
pallid motionless lake, misted, hardly seen, but slender,
    sturdy, indomitable they came again, suddenly the
green stems of daffodils, spurning the rejection of light.
The pale clean stalks, each one a resurrection, each
    one piercing the shroud. Day will command night yet.
The scattering clouds inscribe it. On the bough, the
tight folded buds insist, through mire and flood,
    blossom rises to triumph. Across fields of snow the
fury of colour will riot once more, will flower from
the throat of every bird, one heart singing through
    darkness, to lure the sun, the first dawn that drums
from the core of earth, winter banished by morning.

Airport

I never called you by your name until I left.
There was no need. I had so many others –
private, public, tender, desirous.
A trove of stories, the lustre of old movies,
some Russian novel.
I never called you by your name until you left.

Now, it chimes through empty halls and air
resounding in the rooms we might have
shared.
Through galleries of mirrored strangers
lost
In thronged, deserted streets
lost.
Through glass and rain and blood
its three vowels shriek.
In the hidden chambers of the heart –
where once, unspoken, it pulsed with mine.

I never called you by your name until I left.

There was no need. I had so many others. One
for your pleasured face, another for its sorrows.

Powerscourt

Leaves of amber
fallen –
white gold
the light of winter.
A spider's lace
in new rain,
the sparrow
dazzled.
Figures of stone
observe a garden –
sorrows and glory
stream
unnoticed
at their feet.

An Argument with Fate

Oh look! Look! See how she comes again, striding forth

the voracious old slut, regal, indomitable, in her mantle
of tears and wrack. The cool rapacious teeth agleam. Sure
of her welcome at this altar, the funeral pyre is what she
does best. How well she carries it off, her widow's weed
of regret and self-immolation. She struts her classic chic,
the haggard eye, the so-pale cheek. Death that insatiable

lecher, that greedy old queen has dropped by again to

feel up the living, to fondle and squeeze, to finger fresh
meat. She, the old glutton who never grows an inch fatter
though she laps up everyone else's plate. Fond, amicable
duchess; such a gas, so familiar, the irresistible flatterer.
She's had everyone ever worth knowing. Been to bed with
the lot of them. The great and the wicked, the foolish, the

worse. And, still she won't tell – lips sealed tight as a tomb.

Gorgeous old slag – so gregarious, who even now likes nothing
so well as to stir up a brawl, make her weight felt; scatter
the crowd. See how she taunts and tugs at sermon and wreath,
the coffin's perfumed pall, the valedictories so soft, discreet.
Hear how she hisses and simmers at the lachrymose, festive
mourners gathered to toll the bell, to portray the lost life

sweet and rich, see how they flinch at the sibilant whisper

echoed since childhood grief – 'tell the bloody truth,' she spits
'open up the lid!' With what arrogant panache she plays her
winning card, her cat-among-the-pigeons act, the sharpest
claws unleashed. She must have wearied of it surely, in the
Garden with the snake. But she sets them rowing, one by one,
shakes them by the throat. She has her duty to perform, a

solemn undertaking, her holy writ to read. Oh watch the giddy

dance begin. See how they cut and tear as they bruise and stain
the countenance that most, nearly mirrors theirs. Jealous of
that still warm skin that mocks at hope and wears a lunatic's livid
grin. They have come, they insist, to praise the dead, not cherish
the living damned. But she yawns, our old monarch behind a hand,
tired of her facile victories, her fractious babes, hungry for

breast, gnawing on family marrow. Well, she's done it again as

she always will and has, the last laugh is hers, the final hurrah,
the ultimate breach and wail. Stately and smug she turns to leave.
Who can withstand her art, the lacteal kiss, the black veiled trick?
Her glittering, limitless power? Docile they line themselves up
her pallid children about the grave, bowing to her procuration,
each one weary, wanting their bed. A skeletal hand rests already

on one and every brow – in each pupil see reflected, the patient

stealth they dread. They cannot see or name it but it's born in
their blood, terror stiff as clod or bone. So come, let us bury our
dead, they cry, with ceremony, candle and book. Come slake her
thirst, appease her glance, pay the historic coin, her inevitable,
mortal toll. See how it's done, this ritual, see how the blind
mice run – recall the tribute honoured by each and every forebear.

With arms linked and ears shut, at this feast of putrefaction, with

strewn song and flower, they ring-around a noisy Maypole, all
about the sensual hide, enclosing, stitching tight, the quick,
untutored flesh of any who resist. Oh how she cackles, oh how
she chides as we make merry and sermonise, hear us scorn and
calumniate those few we unearth amongst us, the ardent, whole-
hearted, recklessly blithe, those intransigents stupidly daring to live.

Facing Facts

Look, let's face the facts! Why try to kid ourselves? I've

heard it all. Whatever you do or say, however way you
twist it – it all comes down to the same end, a wooden
box and a hole in the ground. She smiled, my cynical friend
watching the faces drop, hearing the guilty silence fall. She
took the stage and called it like she saw it and she was a
woman who had never worn blinkers. However you
dress it up, she said, whatever fancy clothes you use, music

poetry, fine sentiments, lofty thoughts, high tech and low

Laughter, it all comes down whatever you say to a wooden
box and a hole in the ground. And before that if you're lucky –
as they claim and get a long lease – oh far worse is to find
yourself trapped in living decay, the cunning process of dry
rot, from basement to top, the scaled skin, the useless knees,
the toothless smile, forgetting to wash, the clumsy eating
like a gluttonous babe, the shrunken spine the swollen

hands and feet, the needless questions like a feverish child,

what day is it? What are we doing here? Are we waiting
for Easter or past it? Tell me, where's this I'm living now?
And how many children did I have? Who are we missing?
Don't tease me, please – wasn't there somebody else in the
room a minute ago? And I can't believe it – don't tell me
now that your father is dead! As if I wouldn't have heard it!

Oh, whatever we do or say, my worldly friend continued, it

all comes down to the worms or the oven. Those once elegant
bones burnt and crushed into ashes, the once brilliant mind
shrunken like a slug-eaten cabbage. Oh, let's face it, get real,
whatever you choose to believe or preach it all comes down
to a wooden box and a hole in the ground despite your music
and poetry, travel and learning, high priests and high tech, lofty
thoughts and low jokes, big jobs, flash cars, second homes in

The sun, it all comes down to a crate on a trolley. And friends

and relations standing around drinks in hand, 'a great send off
and everyone came,' they say. It's just as she'd have liked it,
how she wanted to go. After all at her age – what more can you
ask for – a good innings and a merciful release at the finish?
And isn't it great, the rain held off till we got to the lunch?
Oh yes, let's face it, you can't escape facts, my cynical friend
declared bringing the room to a halt, however many flowers or

scented words you strew, however you prettify or prate, in spite

of music and poetry, fine sentiments, lofty thoughts, high tech
and low laughter, drinks in the pub, flash cars and houses, it all
comes down whatever we do to a wooden box and a hole in the
ground. Am I right or am I wrong? Is there anything that I'm
missing? Have any of you something useful to add? Think about
it. Take your time. There's no point in hurry. None of us is going
anywhere important. And relax, remember this is my round.

Signature

Stark
swift
quiet –
sleet
falling –
covers
roof,
fields and
work in
progress

light
snowed in –
labour
solitude,
white sheet.
Of a
sudden –

spring –
its signature
on air
leans out –
melody,
merriment,
news –
petals of
scarlet.

'The Miracle of Death'

Something like birth
death is –
something like making love
a burst of ethereal laughter –
something like joy
is death –
something like finishing
something at last
death is –

Something like starting out
or discovering sorrow –
something like dreaming
of something you dreamed
is death.
Something like waking in
a bed you don't know –

Something like an air
you've never forgotten –
instinct and element
coming together –
each note like colour
in perfect pitch
is death –
each voice parted

Ascending as one.
Something like storm
death is –
like prayer
something like blood –
carried beyond mind,
awe stained
tear swept,
heaven struck –
orgasmic – death is.

Something like the oldest
story on earth —
something so startling,
it takes your breath.
Something like every act
that's happened before
returning
is death
and something never
conceived.

Something like no sight —
heard or touched
that no one alive
can name or can tell
death is —
whether it's how or which
before or after —
whether it closes sense
or opens awareness.
Something like birth
is death
the root of existence —

Something like making love,
like starting out
or like dreaming.
Born of the living —
is death —
into our lifted hands
something like prayer
or storm,
forced from the womb
screaming —
trailing a pulsing cord.

It arrives with life swiftly
or slowly, announcing
itself in labour.
Something like falling awake
something like discovering

sorrow
something like nursing hope –
its image enfolding
the body –
something like a mother
death is –
something like a lover
or muse
a midwife to revelation –

Something like mortality's foil
is death or
something like its contrary –
consider the field
and the lilies –
they who neither toil nor spin
something like these
might death
in all its glory be?
something like falling awake
something like starting out –
something like life's soil –
its seed,
at the flood's bank
a first green stem –
something like transfiguration.

When You Set Out At Last

What can you take with you?
What must you leave behind
when you set out at last?

Gather everything once sought and valued –
all attributes from which you borrowed
weight and stature: success and failure,
reputation, loss, envy and regret.
You will have no further use for them.

Loosed from this little house of troubles
we carry on our backs.

How easy self-surrender then
of being and non-being. Our
earthbound hearts released
to darkness, feel it fall, cast off, an
empty husk: this lifelong freight
of need and craving we heap on
our stooped and bending backs.

This little house of woes, of beauty,
and of grieving.

Leave your shoes at the door.
You have no further use for them.
Barefoot, empty-handed –
step into radiance.

This world unraveling, the universe
is born in you – the truth revealed
that form divides and energy alone
connects.
Pass then across the threshold of
all that separates, shape and time,
space and substance, need and ego
beyond this house of beauty and of
sorrow beloved of our senses.

Arrive to those you wait for.
And those who wait for you.

for Debi O'Hehir in memoriam

Midnight Horses

They came for you at last
where you lay sleeping –
hearing the call they
were born to hear.
Your fierce and lissom horses
galloping
those stallions nervous and quick –
the chestnut mares
of the ebony, flung mane –
galloping –
of the green eyes
flaring –
untamed, keen as
their maker –
the hooves as swift,
the heart as resolute.

At midnight through
dream and phantasm
at last they came
hastening
over hedges and ditch –
hearing the cry
they were born
to hear, stepping
unbridled from the frame
where you had granted
them life,
bowing their heads
for the final time
nostrils flaming –
bareback they
carried you home
across early
morning fields.

for Debi O'Hehir

141

Conspiratorial

Only people
with beautiful faces
walk alone on
Christmas day
in rain,
one dog following
at heel.
They raise
umbrellas high
as they pass by,
they smile into
the gale,
'Hello,' they call
conspiratorial,
'Season's
greetings
to you,'
their cheeks wet,
their eyes
like stars
through mist
ablaze.

Only people
with beautiful faces
invoke the wild
to walk alone
one dog in step.
Tidings of comfort
distant
behind them
on Christmas Day
in storm.

Morning

A warning joist, ice glazed;
light in winter
splits wide the yellow trees –
splays in two the startled limbs
of oak and fern.
It shafts earth's still green
hide, each growing thing, each
frond and blade, agape.
A hidden thrush is tempted into song,
And the holly bush provoked –
flaunts the first crimson fruit.
Even the gilded fox
halts at its lair. Entrapped.
Is it new blood that gleams
on its jaw as it lifts
a shotgun muzzle to the touch?
Flattered by a low, white sun
Its pelt, from head to brush, ablaze.

Shakespeare and Company

Like the bridges wide and capacious over the river far flung fluid their
span paris each one the arch of their backs elegant the seine sinuous
full-flooded forever bending
like the spine of the city the river paris like the bridges the books are
their words over centuries their names spanning like the river turbulent
each one echoing bountiful
like the seine flowing paris centuries crossing like the city of grace full
dame notre dame the bells ringing like the books the words announcing
full of grace   like the river
onwards forever like paris like the bridges the spine stretched bending
like the bridges stretched under our feet to carry us over from far to near
from body to mind
the bridges like the river paris like leaves sepia spreading open like books
like leaves blown
pages like water verdant like paris each drop changing never the same
consciousness streaming on the banks of the river fertile full flowing in
air like song never regretting
in air never ceasing   serpentine paris like the streets its speech under
bridges babel arched over time seamless fast flowing   capacious never
still   like the seine never
finished paris no sentence concluded ever its spine bending like the
bridges never silenced like the words consciousness streaming open
spreading like leaves
on the seine passing all ways like the books passing   like the river
consciousness streaming joyce-less   leaving to arrive   stitched as in
woven the way hemming each
syllable stored the books like the water each drop changing each minute
never twice the same one passing like the river through us through
sense less all ways like the voice
garrulous   swift over   from far to near from body to mind leaving to
arrive   from soul and back each syllable stored   harvested   as in barnes
contentious as in barney
cunning as in cunnard   fertile as violette   senseful as in colette   seductive
in air and song as in anais   serpentine as in toklas its speech under bridges
babel as in wharton   timeless
like the river   never still nor begun   as in rhys   no phrase long winded the
voices   like the bridges   like the books ways passing   like the faces on the
leaves flanner and boyle bryher

anderson   soland   vivienne   pages   turning light on the river   bearing the
titles   all ways   sur le rive gauche as in stein walking   like the   beach tree
wide   its sleeves   sylvan   monnier
her name adding all   ways the words   under the bridges of paris   comme la
rivière passing like the river   en passant   comme le fleuve toujours the
pages of the books   turning
never ceasing never finished comme la rivière ending to begin   like the
river the words   all ways beginning   under the bridges   the books are leaves
flooding words beginning again paris

Atlantic

You wanted me to watch. A dazzled mirror. The low
scooped back, the sinuous purple of your bathing suit
with its oval window, framing, the straw blonde of
skin that shifted like silk over lean muscle, as you
strode long-limbed towards open sea, certain my gaze
followed.

Each high-arched step, your calves like willow, twin
saplings bearing you anointed, queen-like, across a wind-
frosted beach.

I turned my head and walked away, to the far end where
a confusion of dogs and children, played in high-pitched
voices that could seem innocent. In the shallows,
kittiwakes paddled a soft shoe shuffle, herring gulls flew
low, as is their wont, beneath the ribboned, azure cloud
and shrieked a harsh storm warning.

When you came back in your flesh was bruised a livid
crimson. The salt of the Atlantic glittered on your thighs.
You reclaimed the land as one who makes her own, each
inch of earth she walks on. You stood, on the old harbour
pier, your fine-cut heels on cold stone, serene and regal.
You asked me to hold your towel

to screen you while you dressed. Was that the start of it?
Your look? The chill-flushed cheek? In my hands, the dense
white soft cloth, warmed. Seawater like beads of amber
falling from tendrils of your hair.

Grace Notes

But what is it precisely, what is the actual substance, the
    difference between that and this, they ask? Is it not one
sense and one only? Yet again they query, as you labour to
    define, dissect from line to line words once hot that grow chill
as you talk, as you search for a substitute, an approximate near

or far on this perilous journey from origin language, to target.
    You have come to a standstill, stuck fast in the mire, a common
place phrase, has brought you to impasse. The hour is late, paper
    smears the oaken table, they pour another glass of wine, red as
arterial blood. You swallow it in a draft. But what is it exactly

this image, this grist, this irreducible essence that gets lost in
    the process? Water in the mill is what we would say, so let
us say water? Is it not also harmonious? They proffer bread,
    they offer cheese, Catalan ham, the best of the region. To
give you strength they coax, urging you on to one last effort.

You speak then of music, leaning on metaphor, of measure and
    cadence, colouration and pitch, you talk of painting, half shades
and shadowings, of drama and dance, the delicate choreography of
    order and pause, you enlarge and expand, a slip forward or back,
a change of key, a quarter beat, an embellishment. In each form

they exist, do they not, though in different fashion? Brief lines
    embroidered, the pearls of vernacular, the quirks? In dance
yes, in painting or music, of course, clearly, we understand
    but in language, they say, in free verse? You must pin down
these touches that cannot be stated. From the street a church

bell cleaves clear space. Eight chimes travel the wall. You stir
    around the dregs of your wit and gather breath steady and deep.
Is not sense one element only? you ask. More revealing by
    far is the tone, a quality unmistakable in articulation or melody?
The mood, the voice, the turn of phrase. The grace notes, the

rhythm you might say of what passes. At the window, light quails
    from the reach of night. On the white page images cluster,
merge and grow dim. Well, no matter, they say, if for us these
    eloquent little ones do not exist. With so much that is rich in our
idiom have we need of them? They raise their ringing glasses high

and laugh. They pour the last of the wine. Bright pearls spill gleaming
    from the bottle's rim staining the cloth. You smooth it with a hand
It's nothing they say, five beads of crimson on pale linen. But that's
    it, you exclaim, don't you see – the grace notes – exactly! Letters
suspended in silence. A space sculpted about a word – a highlight,

a trick of emphasis, like drops of scarlet on a white ground. I can't
    put it better. They lift their pens, they turn new sheets. This
we begin to comprehend. Perhaps only in poetry, you say, at last,
    gaining momentum, only in poetry these absences elude definition,
an inversion, an undertone, all that is jettisoned in the toil from

one tongue to another. Think of a simile, a comparison, you say,
    finding direction, pressing your foot to the pedal, think of an air,
of song – of traditional singing, listen, for the fine ornamentation,
    the halftone, up or down, a morsel that slips from the grasp,
precarious, perishable, a savour, a scent, a sip, as though passing

fine wine from one mouth to another. All that is forfeit in transit
    from one shore to its neighbour. Quite simply and plainly, between
the jigs and the reels, that's it. Nothing more can be said. At the
    heel of the hunt it's that phrase and no other, a shift, a slide,
a shimmy, a fine touch, a word suspended in silence. A grace note.

For Love of Reading

Black on white
brindled –
face to face
engaged,
line on limb
in life,
the two most
bountiful –
artifact or being
brilliant
the two both –
face to face
engaged,
most vivid,
lost
each one
in the other
one
lost.

March of Mankind

Right now
in a lab somewhere,
in Tokyo, or San Francisco
I don't know,
they have taken the voice of God —
where did they get it? —
and they are printing it out
on a 3D printer.
The robot is standing by
to be uploaded.
Learning to go downstairs
is the tricky part.
She speaks in riddles
they found
when they tested her out.
'Don't grab me so hard'
was the first thing she said.
They're working
on speech production
and hand gestures.
Learning to go upstairs
is the tricky part.
Soon she will begin her perilous
journey to
a supermarket near you.

Montparnasse

'What is the reason, do you think?' she asked, 'that all those

we love but injure forgive us almost readily, however deep
the wound?' Was this remarked at Montparnasse when you
sat on Beckett's tomb leaning on his name for rest, weary
with searching among forgotten graves in the torpor of early
afternoon? The glooming boughs of the Cyprus trees drew
close, suggesting shade. Visitors about the avenues straying
long since departed for their lunch. We had the treasured
grave all to ourselves. In search of it we had wandered for an
hour, until a groundsman came with barrow, mop and broom
to scrub the supine tombstone clear. 'How is it that any person

I have damaged has long since pardoned me?' you asked aloud,

'while those who betrayed me hoard resentment still?' You
stretched on the marble slab and smoothed the moist surface
with your palm. Strange that you should have posed that question
there resting where lay the most cultivated, European poet of despair.
It stirred in me a memory of something else that only came to full
recall much later when you recalled it too. 'Have you heard,' you
asked, 'that Beckett for twenty years or more went to visit London
to meet another woman? And Suzanne knew all about it.' This
last was said, I know at Père Lachaise, one hour on at least from
Montparnasse. The languor of the minutes by then weighed on our

skin like lead, the sun grown harsh as ash. You stood by the grave

of Sidonie Colette and brought fingers to your lips then touched
the tanned brown headstone with a kiss. 'The first and still the
best,' I said. The warden glared beneath his little cap and pointed
to the clock. The iron gate stood wide. 'Is it easier to forgive those
who have sinned against us, do you think than those whom we
have sinned against?' Water in the narrow gutter trickled sluggishly
and brittle. We walked downhill with heavy tread, the guards
impatient at our heels. 'Is it guilt that makes them turn from me?'
We paused for breath. A hounding bell rang out behind us. The street
ahead sloped all the way to Notre Dame. 'Is it shame that makes

them ugly – not remorse? Shame I see stiffen their corpse cold eye?'

Cadiz

Would I recognise you, the moment our gaze
meets? You, my last love, the love of my life.
You the one I passed that November night, as
I hurried from track to train, scuffing my
ankle on the turnstile, platform five at the
Gare de Lyon. Weighted by the baggage I ought
to have left behind me – that you would have
known to leave behind. Was it you who smiled,
offered me your hand before the crowd swept
you into darkness on the other side of my life?

Will I know you at once, the moment my eyes

catch yours again, my lost love? Will I remember
seeing you that morning, walking from the sea
at dawn, the glittering Aegean running from
your thighs. Was it you then who stared me full
in the face, challenging me to what? Before the
oystercatchers left the incoming tide, their
footprints like fossils in wet sand and tourists
flocked to pitch camp, their bought and paid
tranche of paradise. Without hesitation if we were
to pass in the street, would I recognise you, if

I were to hear your voice again? As I heard it

before, once on an August day you have no reason
to recall. Late afternoon, the houses shuttered,
swallows bustling between the spires. An azure
sky hovering in the back streets. You sat by
the western door, a wide-brimmed hat laid in
your lap, to talk to the lace-makers who gathered
by the cathedral steps. It was you, I'm certain
who stopped to admire their labour, the old
women of Cadiz who in the shadow of the square
set out their stalls, embroidered by antique

tradition, their skin, its pattern as intricate as

the white cotton that through dark fingers
skipped and flowed. Wasn't it you who bought
six fine handkerchiefs, you would not use only
so they might know that the timeless self-
effacement of their craft was not for nothing.
Did I hear you offer more than they bargained
for? When you turned to the sun, I saw your
face, its sudden tenderness made you, for an
instant to them more a daughter than a sightseer,
your expression as intimately wrought by time

as theirs, your gaze as clear, as unforgiving.

I remember thinking — in another life — this
woman might be ... but impulses of such kind
we divest ourselves of, do we not? Disown
and leave forgotten in railway stations and hotel
rooms with that novel half-read, the letter
unfinished, the photograph we meant to post,
a record internal, superfluous. Only a voice
snared in sunlight, a race of white linen. Fleeting
tributaries of fancy cumbersome in the everyday.
Tell me why this should happen, you, because I cannot.
Tell me why you, my last, my first love, because I cannot.

Swallow

Hill
field
and
soughing
fir —
still
snow
shrouded.
Somewhere
else
a swallow
readies
sail —
sweet
stealth
of song
and summer.

Artful

Your body is strewn across the pages of old books

cherished or forgotten, indexed or mislaid,
paperbacks that have made their home
on shop window sills and library shelves,
to prop open a door or warm a park bench.

Your body is strewn across the pages of old books

a thousand miles from the rough-hewn desk
where I first made them or from the bed sheets
where you and I in the furnace of early love
conceived them.

Your body is strewn across the pages of old books

your breasts and belly, your silken thighs,
strangers can rifle the leaves, finger your skin,
feast their eyes on sensuality that once revealed
itself for my regard alone.

Your speaking hands have found their way into

the classrooms of school children. No one there
recognised their gestures or felt their supple bones:
'hands that made a silence wherever they touched a
stopping place, the first before love.'
Cherished or mislaid –

your body is strewn across the pages of old books,
on kitchen tables or pillow cases. Pristine or well-
thumbed, artful or negligent, I put it there,
the pages lying open for the eyes of the world to

see, only when certain mine was lost at last to yours.

Words

Is literature the attempt to say in words what cannot be said
in words? Does it seek to
express the ineffable, the amorphous, the banished, to find
voice for exchanges too
exposing for table talk, too intangible for politics, for academic
theses too inchoate?
Is it the last trade, quixotic in effect and intention, to grapple
with the fluid and ambiguous –
to play with language at the cellular basis of matter and
consciousness or to put it
in the prose of every day to feel the unrecognised, to imagine
the unthinkable?
As if one might dissect a
bird in flight, or stall by will the hour in its transit, as if from
spells and potions one
could magic from the air of alphabet, forces both tensile and
compressive and with an
engineer's wands, in precise algebra build an arch of steel from
water and through this alchemy
conjure a bridge sinuous, resilient enough to distribute the load,
to bear us across the torrent
from logic to soul and back again, frayed lathes of reason quaking
at our step, all around us passion's uproar cascading in our ears.

Olive Groves

What I did not know then when we woke on a sleep-

tossed beach in Sardinia and plunged in the same
nude, split-second sense straight into the night-chilled
senseless sea. Or lounging on the sidewalk on Clinton
Street, in an idling Brooklyn hot afternoon, high
as dykes on a very fine bottle of stolen Chablis.

What I did not know then about you in our girlhood –
lovely, besotted, wantonly free, the unique and extra-
ordinary thing about you with me: all night making
love on the night train to Venice until the crimson sun
rising came with us. Or asleep mouth to mouth among

olive groves on Sapphic dusk-spilling evenings in Greece.

Oh no, it was not your ardour or beauty alone that won
me. It was these two and more. One element unregarded
in those head-spinning, negligent days spun before time,
but momentous. I see you now clearly as you were then, in
a sheer, pale silk sarong, or your black dinner-jacket,

cowboy boots and bow tie. Even better, at your best, in
your own bared, tan skin, those breasts, those thighs,
the glance that singed sheets. Those eyes. Not only the
whole of your fervent, feline, felicitous self but one
Thing still finer even than these. In the sepia vision of

retrospect, I see the incomparable, irredeemably you
that you were to me then and now always will be, softly lit
by a thousand flames guttered, I perceive you were that
once in a lifetime one only, the first to be adult and young;
more than that you were in body and spirit the essence –

my bountiful, gorgeous, bedazzled – my own gilded youth.

Possession

We call it having sex as if it were like having
a mortgage or having new shoes or having the flu.
We call it having sex
as if it were like having a break or having a bank
loan or having a job. We used to call it making
love when we knew
love was a thing that needed making. When we
prized the things we made with our hands. Not
only objects
bought and consumed. By the eyes. We call it
having sex. We can have it anywhere, with any
one, at any hour, any pose,
any tool, any price. We can buy it faster than a
pack of cigarettes. We used to call it making love
when we still made friends
made time and made protests, made music and
and made revolution. When we made trouble
made light of it and made peace.
We use to call it making love when we knew any
thing made needed time and attention. When
sensuality was earthed in
the senses, one voice, one scent, one skin at a time.
We used to call it making love when love was a
place we made
with one other who knew that pleasure and pain
and orgasm are verbs. Someone who took joy in
making miracles –
turning flesh and blood into love with their hands.

Rowing from Shore

1.

The first time at the oars,
the last days of childhood
deep as the glimmering
lake – a boy's smile.

2.

Pale clouds at evening
dark skin at dusk,
a swan overhead,
strong as its wing beat
the first stroke of the oar.

3.

On the edge of the old
world, a silver sky
the surge of the prow,
the glance shy.
Each length of the
blade over water –
a youth leaving
boyhood behind.

Parting

The moment I opened the door I saw you were dying
and saw that you knew it too. How was it nobody else
had noticed? Your doctor had said there was no need to

worry, he would drop in again on Monday. But the
moment I opened the door I saw you were dying and
I saw that you knew it too. You looked in the semi-
private care home bed, a companion asleep in a cot
alongside, almost at your best, sitting stacked upright
against a throne of pillows, your hair swept up from
a clear brow. You had your usual air, when facing
any uncertain ground, composed, courageous, ready
to be amused. The only note out of place, the one

physical clue was your colour, across your cheeks and
under your eyes a blue-black stain had risen seeping
like ink under the skin. You looked expectant or was it

absorbed as if you were listening intently to a sound I
couldn't hear. You had never up to this cared for
departures, airports and stations discomfited you but
here, now your face held a tone almost eager. I sat down
on the stiff metal chair by your bedside. I kissed both
your cheeks. Turning slowly in my direction you smiled
but made no reply. I guessed then the effort it took to
stay this balanced and still. As if you were holding some
precious liquid in a glass too shallow knowing any abrupt

motion might spill it. I had never found you not ready to talk.
So I took the family photographs down from the shelf behind
you where I had set them twelve months before. I said aloud

all the names of your children, one by one, coming last to my
own. The youngest I said. You thought that was funny. You
smiled without moving your lips. I told you where each one
was living, which one might get here in time and which might
not. You listened without the least show of surprise. Then
I said the names of your mother, your father and your six

dead siblings. 'They are expecting you, I've sent word. They will have everything ready.' You smiled. I asked if you were thirsty and you said yes. But when I held the plastic beaker to

your mouth the juice ran everywhere staining the front of your new bed jacket. We need more practice at this, I said. We'd better start quickly then, you replied. Your last riposte and you

smiled. But you struggled to bring the words clear. Then, I saw what the trouble was; you were drowning, softly, little by little. I could hear the fluid bubbling in your lungs. Stealthily gaining ground. And I understood all your strength was used to just to keep your head above water. Does it hurt, I asked you. Yes, you said. Where? Everywhere, you answered and smiled. A memory came to mind, in a slip of association, a spring tide rising, gushing into the harbour, the one our house overlooked, the one where you brought us all up. Each year it rose without

warning submerging small boats at anchor, sinking from sight the big pier, as we called it in a gush of voracious green spume. 'Are you hungry,' I asked. 'A little,' you said. I searched

about in the locker for the last packet of citrus fruit jellies, your favourites. We had been told you must have nothing by mouth but what the hell, I said and laughed. 'Yes,' you replied. Your smile was close to laughter. Gingerly, at the corner of your mouth I slipped them in, the glossy bright sweets between dry parted lips. Delightful and delicious you managed to say, a phrase you had taken to in the last months when a visitor brought you chocolate or an ice-cream cone all to yourself. The tears that ran from my eyes were so hot they scorched a

path that stayed long after. I wiped my face with the edge of your sheet. You smiled. Delightful and delicious. The water babbling under each word carried them up like balloons to sway in the air

above your bed. But though you could not harness the sounds, it was clear from all your responses that here at the grave's kerb your wits had recovered their senses. Perfectly lucid now, you gazed at the book by your locker. I knew you wanted to say as we did every day until this, one or two of the poems that by some

trick had survived the ravage of body and brain. One was by
Dickinson and one was by Shelley: *'Higher still and higher
From the earth thou springest   Like a cloud of fire   The blue
deep thou wingest.'* At times we mixed their lines together. None

but your re-ordered mind would see how they mirrored each
other. *'Hope is the thing with feathers   That perches in the
soul,   And sings the tune without the words,   And never stops at*

all.' In equal esteem you held the two, prizing as you did
faith, irony, awe, a sense of the absurd. You made one last
great effort then, raising your shoulders up from the pillows,
you struggled to give utterance, a sentence, twice, three times
the particles running each which way like beads scattered.
Once more you tried, you grasped my wrist, this time two
syllables broke free 'Writing' I heard you say and once more
'Writing,' with a harsh exhalation of breath. I settled you back
in your eyrie of cushions as best as I could. You wanted to lie

flat facing the ceiling. I drew the curtain tight round the bed.
The old lady next to us made no stir, lost in her own drugged
slumber death was no bother. And neither, amazing, was I in

the least awkward or frightened. Whatever happened when
we two were together seemed a part of the natural and what
was most hard to endure we found a way to make bearable. And
this famous scene, this dying now, was only one more thing
we had to get right between us. The drapes drawn close brought
some quiet, suggested rest, 'I'll let you sleep for a bit. I'll get
something to eat and come again in an hour.' When you heard
this you opened your eyes. You smiled. You put out your hand
to touch my face. You intended to stroke it I know but you

couldn't adjust the speed or the force. Your open palm slapped
my cheek. Then all the way slowly down it slid from temple to
jaw. Ten times your hand rose, and smote my face, ten times it

slipped down heavy from temple to chin, ten times it slid down,
ten times. The rhythm, the rough insistence of it, seemed to
be saying: 'Remember this, remember this. Until we meet again.
Remember this.' The pressure sounded through my veins.

With each clumsy blow that fell, you fixed on me a regard so
luminous and calm it shocked. It nearly stopped my heart.
Greater even than I had guessed, and I had always known –
was the ardour I saw stand in your eyes. As if all the love you
had kept stored since first you carried me, was gathered up,

each day and year of it, and given back as legacy in that
marveling, speechless gaze. Was it imagination to feel that its
light journeyed already from a space beyond us both? At last,

I caught your wrist, held it still. 'You're hurting me,' I murmured.
You dropped you arm and smiled, nearly the last smile you would
ever give. I kissed your forehead. I smoothed your hair. How
strange I thought that in this long uncertain passage not once had
you been fearful or sad, joy was the element you entered and shared,
I knew even then I would come to count it the most precious of
the things you left behind you. I felt also a change in you, a subtle
reversion of roles, for the first time in I don't know how long, you
were a parent again, a lifetime's sense of protection reborn. To

please you and from an old habit I whispered the words of the Salve
Regina. You followed me silently note by note. 'Turn then most
gracious advocate thine eyes of mercy towards us and after this our

exile show unto us the blessed fruit of thy womb.' I stopped there
not wanting Jesus to get the ultimate credit as usual. You noticed of
course and smiled. I spoke then, though I did not know it, the final
words I would speak on this earth as a daughter, words I used to
ask for from the dark when I heard you coming up the stairs to say
goodnight, 'See you in the morning, please God.' You had thought
Joyce was wrong to refuse his mother and so did I. You smiled
when you heard the last phrase and closed your eyes. I leaned my
head on your bed and wept. Arms held sentinel at your side, you

snored in your sleep like a child with a cold and did not move again.

MARY DORCEY is a critically acclaimed Irish poet, short story writer and novelist. She won the Rooney Prize for Irish Literature in 1990 for her short story collection *A Noise from the Woodshed*. Her poetry and fiction is researched and taught internationally at universities throughout the United States, Canada and Europe. The subject of countless academic critiques and theses, it has been anthologised in more than one hundred collections. She is a member of Aosdána, the Irish Academy of Writers and Artists and is a Research Associate at Trinity College where for seven years she led seminars at the Centre for Gender and Women's Studies. The first Irish woman in history to advocate for LGBT rights, she is a lifelong activist for gay and women's rights. Founder member of 'Irish Women United,' 'The Sexual Liberation Movement,' and 'Women for Radical Change.' Her poetry is taught in schools at O-Level in Britain and on the Irish Junior Certificate. She has lived in England, the USA, France, Japan, Italy and Spain. She has published eight previous books: *Kindling* (Onlywomen Press, 1982); *A Noise from the Woodshed* (Onlywomen Press, 1987); *Moving into the Space Cleared by our Mothers* (Salmon Poetry, 1991); *Scarlet O'Hara* (Onlywomen Press, 1993); *The River that Carries me* (Salmon Poetry, 1995); *Biography of Desire* (Poolbeg, 1997); *Like Joy in Season, like Sorrow* (Salmon Poetry, 2001); and *Perhaps the Heart is Constant after All* (Salmon Poetry, 2012). She is currently completing a collection of novellas: *The Good Father*. She lives in Wicklow, Ireland.